T0322250

A Love of Eating

To our Mums for giving us
the love of eating

A Love of Eating

Lucy Carr-Ellison
& Jemima Jones

◨ SQUARE PEG

Contents

Foreword:
The
Photographic
Kitchen

When I first met Lucy she must have been in her teens. Like all teenagers she was trying to figure out her path in life and was considering taking up photography. She came and helped out on an Italian Vogue fashion shoot where I was taking a picture of Lily Cole dressed as bait and tackle on a giant fishing hook suspended over a Northumbrian river.

Lucy soon started to take a lot of pictures of her own which she kept in a box. She photographed friends, family and boyfriends. The pictures were good and really seemed to be going somewhere, but to support yourself as a young photographer starting out is hard, so she decided to help out in the kitchen, catering for the crew on photographic shoots. One thing led to another and eventually she met Jemima; they joined forces and cooked for all my crew, who were always hungry after the very early starts fashion photography demands. Jemima was the perfect addition to the tarty duo, chattering away serving spicy eggs for breakfast or slow cooked lamb for lunch on chilly days out on location. The two working together have come from cooking dishes on a camp stove out on a location shoot, to the recipes in this book.

My mother used to write cookbooks so I grew up constantly trawling through the market hunting for the right this, or the right that. We'd go a long way to get Seville oranges or whatever the target of the ingredient hunt was and I remember my Mum's utter joy in that quest. Once we had found what she wanted, it was swung round and round in a brown paper bag, dropped in the wicker basket and hauled back to the kitchen for grating, squeezing, boiling then reducing, or whisking, mixing, folding then baking…

Cooking is all about the right ingredients… And taking photographs is very much like cooking.

I obsess about sniffing out the ingredients that combine to create a photograph. I'll go a long way, get up very early, and stay up very late, to seek out a specific light, colour, backdrop, animal, mineral or vegetable that I see as part of a magical combination that articulates a mood in my belly.

The book you are now about to read is a love letter to that universal joy of seeking out the right ingredients. That same discernment, obsession and taste that lies behind a great photograph is just as relevant here, freshly baked in Lucy and Jemima's oven and served as a Tart.

Tim Walker
London, 2018

The story of Tart is really all about the beginning of a friendship.

In 2010 we were both in our early twenties and living in the East Village in New York – Lucy was studying photography and Jemima interning at *Vanity Fair*. We were having a great time: working hard and taking full advantage of the incredible restaurant culture there. We were put in touch by a mutual friend and met for the first time on the Lower East Side – Lucy was running late from having a piercing done and caught Jemima in the nick of time – we immediately got on… not least because of our shared obsession with food. We would venture all over the city to try out new restaurants, pop-ups, shops and markets, captivated by the constantly evolving scene, and taking every opportunity to try new dishes and ingredients.

When we came back to London a few years later, we were buzzing from our experience. Happily, we found that a food revolution was taking place in the UK. People had begun to put more thought into the quality of the food they ate, and good food was more popular than ever. But we realised that one thing was missing. When we'd been together on photoshoots in New York, we were always struck by the amazing, fresh, healthy food on offer – it was proper food, made by hand, and a long way from the dry sandwiches and wilted salads you would be faced with in the UK. We realised that what was missing was a boutique-style catering company that made wholesome, attractive food that people actually wanted to eat – and we were the people to do it. We decided to set up Tart.

In a whirlwind of early mornings and long days of planning and preparation, we went from enthusiastic foodies who loved to cook delicious feasts for friends and family, to professional cooks running on-site catering kitchens – everywhere from a horsebox in the countryside to a tiny minimalist studio in the city. But even though we were now cooking for bigger groups (around 40 or 50), it was important to us to create a cosy atmosphere for everyone to come together, eat and enjoy their time off. We have always made everything fresh from scratch, in situ, and this really helps not only to create great tasting food, but to inspire a sense of togetherness too. We think hard about the variety and presentation of our food. Models want to eat well, feel good and look good, but we also cater for a whole crew who need something satisfying and sustaining. We plan our menus with this in mind, providing an assortment of sharing platters that are well balanced and seasonal, but nourishing too. We are constantly inspired by our travels, always picking up ideas from the ingredients, techniques and dishes we encounter on trips and holidays, the things that make food delicious and unusual. At Tart our ethos is to take the flavours and vibrancy characteristic of our home cooking and translate it into something bigger in scale, but applying the same thought and care that makes sharing a meal together so special.

More recently, we have created a two-month pop-up restaurant in west London, started a weekly recipe column in the *Evening Standard*'s *ES Magazine* and are looking at opening a more permanent venue soon. These new ventures have been amazing experiences. Writing our column each week is a gift – it's a fantastic opportunity to practise and develop our dishes, but it has also allowed us to understand how to write good, simple recipes that work well. Getting them down on paper and putting ourselves in the place of the home cook means we really think about all

of their different components – the ingredients, techniques, how things can be made simpler or easier, or where a recipe needs a little final something.

Running the pop-up gave us an opportunity to learn, too. It was a completely different space to cook in and gave us insight into how a busy restaurant works. We had to look at presenting individual plates and providing a changing menu, and this made us recognise even more the need for delicious and interesting food that was also easy to make. Running a catering company and a restaurant has enhanced our love of seasonal and local produce, and recognition of how much tastier, more economical and environmentally responsible it is. When you are buying ingredients to cook with on a regular basis, it's not a luxury to buy seasonally – it just makes sense. It's something that has been central to our way of eating for a long time. We are both based in London, but a significant amount of our time is spent in the countryside – Lucy having grown up in Northumberland on her family farm and Jemima having a little farm in Somerset. We often come back from nurturing family weekends with baskets of fruit and vegetables. Using fresh produce at its peak, especially if it has been picked nearby (or by us!), is something we love to do, and the people who eat our food love it too.

However, while our experiences and background have been hugely important in the creating of Tart, and have helped to form our ethos, most of all we just want cooking to be fun and easy. It doesn't need to be taken too seriously! Whether making something quick at home for yourself or whipping up a feast for hordes of people, it should be enjoyable, not stressful. We work long, hard days and when we come home we want to cook easy, healthy, feel-good recipes that are also affordable. This is where a lot of our one-pot wonders come in. We want to feel satisfied, without making a whole

lot of mess, so being able to whack a lot of things from the fridge into a pot, pour wine and stock over it and then go and have a bath is an easy treat. We approach cooking in a light-hearted way, because we want to enjoy what we do and to enjoy our lives. For this reason we don't condemn alcohol, cheese or puddings: everything in moderation is our motto.

This book is about our approach to cooking. It is about the joy of sharing and interacting and the excitement of new flavours, about the beauty of colour, texture and simplicity, and the importance of seasonality and good produce. More than anything it is about the pure pleasure of creating a delicious meal, simply and easily, for yourself and those you love.

art London hits a food milestone

for the Evening Standard Mag

1 bag ba...
2 large avoco...
½ jar toma...
1 small bag,
25g toasted

3 tbsp olive...
½ lemon ju...
salt + pe...

arrange
platter.
2. mix
season
over left
a
e

JO MALONE
LONDON

Lucy,
Thank you
for everything,

TART LONDON

Jemima Jones
and Lucy Carr-Ellison

ES Magazine CONVERSE

"TART .....
art and tarta s
Our favourite ton shoot cooks

Our favourite Shoot Caterer cook "

Menu

December 6th

Starter
Tuna Ceviche

Main
Persian Chicken
with Pistachios and...
OR
Crab Ravioli
with lemon and sage...

Dessert

MULBERRY

SPRING CRAB SALAD WITH LEMON CREME FRAICHE AND EDIBLE FLO...
WHITE BEAN AND ROSEMARY PUREE WITH GOLDEN CANDY, ENGLISH BEETROOTS AN...
LAMB CUTLETS WITH ROSE HARISSA OR SALSA VERDE
SPRING PEAS, BEANS, EDAMAME AND MINT
SEA KALE, SORREL AND SPINACH
BURRATA, ROCKET, CHILLI, BASIL
BROCCOLI WITH OPTIONAL RAW CASHEW DRESSING

Menu Planning
The Tart Checklist

Putting a menu together can seem daunting, sitting at the kitchen table in a sea of open cookbooks with a blank notepad. Where do you start?

We have never been a catering company that has a generic list of dishes to send to clients – we create every menu especially for each client, and we have never done the same menu twice. We have to deal with menu planning on a daily basis and we find it much easier to formulate a plan if we go through our 'Tart checklist'. Whether we are catering for a team of 100 or for six friends we approach it in the same way – creating a colourful and delicious spread of mix-and-match dishes that people can dig into. We like to look at all of our menus in this way, whether at work or at home, rather than using the same old formula of starter, main and dessert. Though even if you do have those elements, perhaps for a more formal dinner party, you can build the menu in the same way – looking at the meal as a whole and making sure you tick off each part of the checklist at some point. Hopefully taking these same steps will help you to put together terrific menus, too.

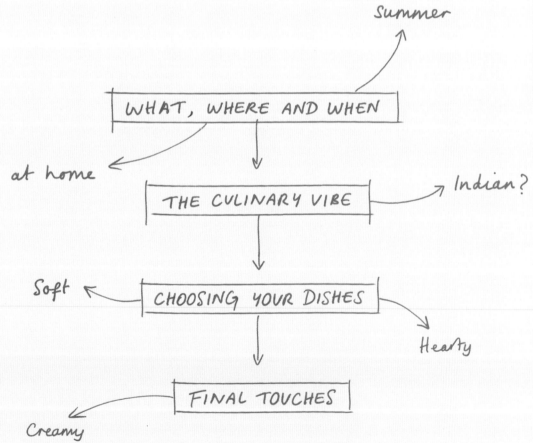

Summer

WHAT, WHERE AND WHEN

at home

THE CULINARY VIBE → Indian?

Soft ← CHOOSING YOUR DISHES → Hearty

FINAL TOUCHES

Creamy

What, Where and When

Before really getting into the specifics of the menu, we always start with 'what, where and when'. Quickly answering these questions will pave your way.

What: what is the event you're cooking for? What's the reason for getting together? Is it a relaxed and intimate family gathering, a more formal event such as an anniversary, a fun brunch or a big birthday bash? Thinking about this first will help you focus on the style and atmosphere you want to go for – whether you want it stylish and refined or loud and fun.

Where: where are you going to be? Are you hosting in your familiar kitchen or eating at someone else's home? Is it perhaps outside – with a barbecue, or a picnic by the sea? Think about the practicalities of where you will be – whether you have the use of a kitchen, how big your prep area will be, what the weather might be like and if the food will have to keep outside of a fridge for a long time.

When: what time of day will it be? Which season? Will you be eating al fresco on a balmy June evening or snuggled by the fire on a drizzly autumnal afternoon? Think about the weather, temperature, light and mood. How will people be feeling at that time of day, or time of year?

Once you have thought about all of these elements, it's time to get to work on the plan.

The Culinary Vibe

You know the what, where and when for your event, occasion or meal. Now you need to think about your culinary vibe. Of course you can mix and match, but we always find it helps to have an idea of the kind of cooking you want to do. Will it be modern British? Japanese, Korean, Thai…or even Asian fusion? Italian, Indian, Mexican…perhaps something new you've been wanting to try, like Eastern European or Greek? Thinking about this will clear your head and help you hone in on which dishes to choose. Pick one as the starting point, and then you can think about the individual components of the meal.

Choosing Your Dishes

We usually base our menus on 5–7 dishes for sharing, even for small numbers, as it is nice to have a variety. If the menu is simple, just make the smaller dishes super simple too. They could be something as easy as a bowl of lightly spiced yoghurt, a cucumber salad or a crunchy seed topping. However, even preparing 3–4 components rather than your usual two can make such a difference. Don't overstretch yourself by planning too much.

Depending on the answer to the 'where' question we usually go for 1–2 hot 'main' dishes, with the rest room temperature or cold dishes. Even if your location is outside you could still provide a hot option – just pack a camping stove, plan something easy to heat up and make it in advance. Otherwise, think of something that is going to be the star of the show. For the main dishes, we usually have a meat or fish dish and a vegetarian option, so everyone can have a bit.

After choosing your hot main dish (or dishes), think about what will go with them.

Hearty: make sure there's something carby and filling on the menu – you want to keep those empty tummies happy! Grains, pasta, beans, pulses, rice and potatoes all fit in this section.

Crunchy: now think about the texture of your meal. You have hot and you have hearty, so you want something fresh and crunchy, too. Perhaps a raw salad or some crisp steamed vegetables.

Soft: you have your crunchy component, so go for a softer element too – maybe something roasted? Roasted food doesn't have to be hot – you can easily do this in advance and serve it cold with a delicious dressing.

Colour: review your choices so far. Are all your dishes looking the same? Pick something that is going to be loud and colourful to pull your spread together.

By now you will be up to 6 dishes. What could be the final cherry on the cake? A simple garden salad? A dip or sauce? A small bite such as a croqueta? A fun bruschetta?

Final Touches

Take a look at your plan as a whole – does it feel balanced and have a nice flow? You might want to start tweaking, thinking about the following:

Texture: do you want to add an extra crunch, perhaps a seed or a chopped nut?

Taste: do you want to add a herb?

Creaminess: do you want to add a spiced yoghurt or a crumbled cheese for a mellow tang?

Sweetness: do you want to add a drizzle of honey or a maple-glazed nut?

Sourness: do you want to add dried cranberry or sour cherry?

Freshness: do you need another squeeze of lemon or lime?

Colour: do you want to add a bright garnish or blushing nasturtium flower?

Spice: do you need to add a kick of chilli or a crushed spice?

And now you're done! Have a glass of wine, relax and write your shopping list.

WHAT : a cosy supper with friends
WHERE : at home
WHEN : a late summer evening
CULINARY VIBE : South Indian

Crunchy Salad

A fresh squeeze of lime

Colour from the green chutney

A final sprinkle of herbs

Soft roasted cauliflower

Hearty dosa

Creamy spiced yoghurt

Extra spice from the tarka

A drizzle of sweet honey

Extra crunch and texture from curry leaves and crispy garlic

One hot main dish

A Few Suggested Menus

We're all about putting on a big, colourful spread that's fun to cook and fun to eat, so we would encourage you to mix and match from whichever recipes take your fancy, to create whatever type of menu you need. That being said, we know that sometimes you just need a little inspiration, so we've put together a few sample menus here that you might like to try. These are well balanced, providing a good variety of tastes, textures and colours.

Lunch

Pea, Courgette and Basil Soup (see page 145)

Roast Tomato and Harissa Tart (see page 92)

Quinoa with Avocado, Peas and Crispy Kale (see page 38 – leave out the egg)

Blistered Courgette with Feta, Pomegranate and Dill (see page 123)

Jalapeño, Cashew and Avocado Dip (see page 256)

A green salad with mustard dressing

———

Lamb Koftas with Smoky Tomato Sauce and Mint Yoghurt (see page 218)

Flatbreads (see page 265)

Roast Sweet Potatoes with Marsala Wine, Orange and Sumac Yoghurt (see page 134)

Saffron Roasted Peppers and Tomatoes, Crispy Chickpeas and Buckwheat with Labneh (see page 74)

Crunchy steamed green beans with Sweet Tahini Ginger Dressing (see page 257)

Shaved Brussels Sprouts with Pine Nuts and Goats' Cheese (see page 104)

Casual Dinner

Truffle Polenta Balls (see page 63)

Flattened Griddle Lamb Chops with Rosemary Borlotti Beans and Wilted Spinach (see page 214)

Baked Ricotta with Mixed Tomatoes (see page 120)

Crispy Artichoke Salad with Capers and Parmesan (see page 98)

A simple rocket salad with a lemony dressing

———

Fun Entertaining

Flatbread Pizzas (see pages 86)

Raw Courgettes with Broad Beans and Mint (see page 108 – leave out the mozzarella)

Smoked Tomatoes, Burrata and Basil Oil (see page 111)

Artichoke Dip (see page 58)

A fresh garden salad

———

Restorative Shiitake Mushroom Broth (see page 140)

Easy Chicken and Pickled Ginger Gyozas (see page 77)

Seared Fillet of Beef Carpaccio with Crunchy Greens, Crispy Shallots and Garlic and a Vietnamese Dressing (see page 113)

Crispy Kale with Tahini and Honey (see page 120)

Pickled Cucumbers (see page 200)

Smoky Harissa or Sichuan Oil (see pages 259–260)

Breakfast
and Brunch

Breakfast is most definitely our thing.

Adelle Davis, America's iconic author and nutritionist, insisted that we ought to 'eat breakfast like a king, lunch like a prince, and dinner like a pauper'. We're told by dieticians and yogis alike that our digestion is most fired up first thing in the morning. What better justification for our love of a delicious, extravagant breakfast?

We met in our early twenties in New York – the city that opened our eyes to how good breakfast and brunch really can be – and as two morning people, we spent the next few months cultivating our love of this most important of meals. At that time London had not properly cottoned on to brunch, and the best you could hope for was a greasy spoon fry-up of the *Withnail and I* variety. Whether jaded from the night before or shining our halos after a yoga class, breakfast is always a joyful moment in the day for us, and missing it is a gloomy prospect.

But we don't only take breakfast inspiration from New York. All of America does breakfast extremely well – classic pancakes stacked high and dripping with maple syrup, the best crispy streaky bacon in the world and fresh orange juice by the pint. The French have a different take, preferring delicate buttery croissants, pastries and fresh fruit washed down by excellent coffee. Breakfast in India is something special, too, with sizzling hot chapatis, spicy eggs cooked any which way with chilli, coriander and tomato, and soothing mango lassies.

Breakfast is most definitely our thing. Our job has consisted of many mornings getting up early and preparing breakfasts on fashion and film shoots – one big long table with fantastic spreads, from interactive egg stations and warm pastries to bircher muesli, granola pots and compotes. We love the endless (and often overlooked) possibilities of breakfast. We have even been written about in the press as 'the girls popular for their eggs', so this chapter was a pleasure for us to put together. We always buy eggs from free-range (or, better, organically raised) hens. We love the Cotswold Legbar eggs in particular – we are possibly biased due to their pretty blue shells, but these always seem to have the brightest, most delicious, rich golden yolks as well.

There is something for all different starts to the day in this chapter – for a more relaxed leisurely one you can try our Goan Baked Eggs or indulgent Tarragon, Ricotta and Parmesan Dippy Eggs, or for quick on-the-go breakfasts there are sweet and sharp bowls like our signature granola or poached rhubarb. Breakfast is simply an unmissable opportunity to start the day well.

Morning Shots

Tart's Granola

Golden Mylk Porridge

Poached Rhubarb with Elderflower

Poached Plums with Star Anise and Cinnamon

Goan Baked Eggs

Tarragon, Ricotta and Parmesan Dippy Eggs

Quinoa and a Poached Egg

Celeriac and Smoked Ham Rösti

Mexican Green Eggs

Turkish Poached Eggs

Spring Green Bruschetta

Spiced Sweet Potato Pancakes

Banana and Oat Pancakes

Pumpkin, Cinnamon and Pecan Muffins

Morning Shots

These pack a punch and will most certainly wake you up in the morning – brilliant for getting the metabolism going. If you would prefer to have one of these recipes as a wake-up juice rather than a shot, add freshly squeezed orange juice to The Lemony One, coconut water to The Berry One or a few apples to The Green One.

All these recipes serve 4.

The Lemony One

juice of 1 lemon
¼ teaspoon ground turmeric
2 teaspoons peeled and grated fresh ginger
1 teaspoon apple cider vinegar (optional)
½ teaspoon cayenne pepper
1 teaspoon honey (preferably raw)

Lemon, cayenne and apple cider vinegar are a top alkalising combo as well as a metabolism booster, plus ginger aids digestion. Turmeric helps the immune system and is anti-inflammatory. Honey is antibacterial, anti-inflammatory and a good source of antioxidants, as well as being a much-needed hit of sweetness when combined with the rest of the ingredients. Mix all the ingredients together and serve.

The Berry One

1 punnet (200g) blueberries
75g blackberries
seeds of 1 pomegranate
½ lime
½ red bird's eye chilli

This is a great energising shot to get you started on your day: a good hit of antioxidants and vitality. A shot is concentrated, which means the nutrients enter your system faster. Put all the ingredients into a juicer and juice together.

The Green One

large handful of kale
1 bulb fennel, quartered
1 cucumber
½ bunch of coriander
½ bunch of mint
½ lemon
5cm piece of fresh ginger, peeled

Green juices have turned into a bit of a trend, one that we have started to tire of. However, they are a very efficient way of spiking your system with healthy ingredients, and improving your mood too. Lucy has never been a huge fan of a big glass of green liquid, so this is a great way of shooting it quickly. You can really use whatever greens you prefer: spinach works instead of kale. Put all the ingredients into a juicer and juice together.

Tart's Granola

Granola is one of the most rewarding things to bake, from stirring the big bowl of grains, nuts and seeds to the comforting smell wafting out of the oven, and ending with the best monthly supply of morning crunch. We love to make our own – it's much healthier and more delicious than the shop-bought stuff, cutting out unnecessary sugar and additives. Try to find old-fashioned oats rather than instant oats, as these are better for you, slowly releasing energy throughout your morning.

The perfect granola is different for everyone. We enjoy a nutty and seedy mix, pecans being a must-add as they take on a wonderful texture when baked. There are no set rules to the recipe below – add and subtract as you like. More often than not it's about using up the half-emptied bags of nuts and seeds in our cupboards. In winter we like to add spices like cinnamon and nutmeg as well as citrus zest. Occasionally we also like to play around with chocolate and nut butters – you can add cocoa powder along with the dry ingredients before baking, but add chocolate chips when the granola has cooled – this is yummmmaa when mixed with hot almond milk (or a milk of your choice).

1. Preheat the oven to 150°C/gas 2.

2. Put the oats and any other grains, seeds, nuts and sea salt into a large mixing bowl and stir together.

3. Melt the coconut oil, maple syrup and honey together in a pan over a medium heat. When it starts to bubble remove from the heat and slowly pour over the dry ingredients, stirring with a wooden spoon as you go.

4. Tip the granola onto a large baking tray, spreading it out evenly. Bake for 30–40 minutes, stirring every 10 minutes, until everything is golden. After 20 minutes add the coconut chips (this is to make sure they don't burn).

5. Remove from the oven and leave to cool on the baking tray. Once cooled, store the granola in airtight jars – it will keep for at least a month.

Makes 2 big jars

250g jumbo oats (or you could do half and half with another grain like spelt flakes, barley, quinoa or even bran flakes)

80g each of pumpkin seeds, linseeds, sunflower seeds, sesame seeds

200g (approx.) each of bigger nuts such as pecans, almonds, cashews, roughly chopped

100g (approx.) each of smaller nuts such as pistachios, hazelnuts and macadamia

pinch of sea salt

80g coconut oil

120ml maple syrup

2 tablespoons honey

80g coconut chips

Dehydrated fruit is a delicious and incredibly pretty addition to this granola. We use a dehydrator, but you can use an oven set at the lowest temperature, ideally no more than 50°C. Slice the fruit lengthways and place so the pieces are not overlapping on sheets of baking paper. Dry out in the oven for about 4 hours. Our favourite fruits to dehydrate are raspberries, strawberries and figs.

Golden Mylk Porridge

Golden mylk is a miracle worker. Turmeric, the vital ingredient here, has been used in Chinese and Indian medicine for thousands of years for many reasons – it helps the immune system, is soothing for the digestion, cleanses the liver and helps with arthritis; it is anti-inflammatory as well as having many other potentially therapeutic benefits. With turmeric it is all about the curcumin, the substance which gives it its wonderful golden colour; it loses its potency slightly when dried, so if you can get your hands on fresh turmeric then so much the better. Wear gloves if you are using fresh turmeric as it stains badly and you'll end up looking like an old chain-smoker. Adding a little black pepper to the mix helps your body absorb the turmeric.

But it's not only the turmeric in golden mylk that makes it so powerful. Raw honey is fantastic; loaded with vitamins and minerals, it soothes a sore throat and also boosts the immune system. If it is locally sourced it can help to protect against tiresome allergies such as hay fever, and as its natural sugars are easily absorbed, it is the perfect early morning fuel. The fat in the coconut milk also slows the release of any sugars, making it a sustainable choice for your energy levels, and will help fill you up so that you do not overeat during the day. It is also a great way to replenish your electrolytes, especially for those doing exercise or running around all day! Cinnamon, too, is loaded with antioxidants, is anti-inflammatory, lowers blood sugars and helps fight bacterial and fungal infections.

You can, as most do, drink the golden mylk as a soothing drink (which is especially good before bed) but by adding porridge oats we make it into a healthy, hearty breakfast.

*Serves 1, generously
(or makes 2 small bowls)*

50g porridge oats
300ml coconut milk
thumb-sized piece of fresh
  turmeric, peeled and grated (or
  1 teaspoon ground turmeric)
1 cinnamon stick
squeeze of honey
  (preferably raw)
black pepper (optional)

TO SERVE (OPTIONAL)
natural yoghurt
fresh fruit

1. Put the oats into a small pan with the coconut milk, turmeric, cinnamon and honey and place over a medium heat. Bring to a simmer and cook gently for 4–5 minutes, stirring occasionally.

2. Add a grind of black pepper, if liked, and serve. It's nice with a dollop of yoghurt on the top and a few berries or slices of fruit.

Poached Rhubarb with Elderflower

Rhubarb – the prettiest vegetable of them all (for they are in fact a vegetable). Early forced rhubarb brings such happiness, the bright pink stems forcing their way through those grey months. This is a staple that we make as soon as we are able and right through the season. We mostly serve it for breakfast with crunchy Tart's Granola and yoghurt (see page 29), but we also use it a lot in desserts – it is very good with (or in) something creamy!

Keep an eye on the rhubarb when poaching – if it overcooks it turns into a stringy mess. You want the rhubarb to be soft, but still have a very slight bite to it.

Serves 6–8

400g rhubarb, cut into
  5cm batons
250ml water
60g honey
½ vanilla pod, split in half
3–4 tablespoons elderflower
  cordial

1. Preheat the oven to 180°C/gas 4 and arrange the rhubarb batons in a suitable ovenproof dish.
2. Put the water into a small pan with the honey, vanilla and elderflower cordial and bring to the boil. Pour this syrup over the rhubarb and then put into the oven for 15 minutes, until just cooked. Remove from the oven and set aside to cool.
3. Store in an airtight container in the fridge – it will last for a week.

Poached Plums with Star Anise and Cinnamon

We have been serving these delicious spiced plums for years – usually early in the morning to a big photographic crew. They are lovely when paired with a comforting hot bowl of porridge. We also use it to accompany desserts – it's very good with the panna cotta on page 230, the plums giving it a Christmassy feel.

Serves 10–12

8 plums, halved and stoned
250ml water
1 orange, pared rind and juice
2 star anise
3 cloves
2 cinnamon sticks
2.5cm piece of fresh ginger,
  thinly sliced into rounds
1 vanilla pod, split in half
  and seeds scraped out (or 2
  teaspoons good vanilla extract)
juice of ¼ lemon
2 tablespoons soft light
  brown sugar

1. Preheat the oven to 200°C/gas 6 and line a roasting tin or dish that will hold the plums snugly with baking paper. Arrange the plums in the dish, cut side up.
2. Put the water, orange rind and juice, spices, ginger and vanilla into a pan and add a squeeze of lemon juice. Bring to the boil, then reduce the heat and simmer for about 10 minutes to make an infused syrup.
3. Pour the hot liquid over the plums, poking the spices around each one. Sprinkle over the brown sugar and then put into the oven to roast for 30 minutes, or until the plums are tender, but still keeping their form.
4. Allow to cool before storing in the fridge in an airtight container.

Rhubarb and ginger
go very well together
– try adding some
grated fresh ginger
to the syrup mix
and serving it with
a creamy dessert
like panna cotta.
You can also add
other spices, such as
cardamom, cloves,
star anise or bay
leaves, or a dash of
orange juice instead
of the elderflower.

Goan Baked Eggs

Brunch is – and should be – about celebrating the enjoyment of eating. We like to indulge in a multi-course brunch, especially when everything is spread down the table to share. This usually occurs once a week, at the weekend. Often you want something a little more than your typical eggs – you want something flavoursome and exciting. This is a dish created for just such an occasion, inspired by our love of India.

Serves 2

2 tablespoons coconut oil

2 shallots, thinly sliced

2 cloves garlic, thinly sliced

thumb-sized piece of fresh ginger, peeled and grated

small bunch of coriander, stalks finely chopped and leaves kept whole

1 x 400g tin chopped tomatoes

2 teaspoons maple syrup

½ aubergine, cut into 1cm cubes

handful of okra, sliced lengthways

1 tablespoon ground turmeric

handful of spinach

4 eggs

1 red chilli, thinly sliced

1 lime, quartered

naan bread or flatbreads, to serve (see page 265 for our homemade flatbreads)

FOR THE SPICE MIX
1 tablespoon cumin seeds
1 tablespoon coriander seeds
1 cinnamon stick
1 tablespoon mustard seeds

FOR THE YOGHURT DRESSING
4 tablespoons natural yoghurt
1 lime, zest and juice
½ red onion, finely chopped
salt

FOR THE SPICY OIL
1 tablespoon salted butter
pinch of chilli flakes

1. Preheat the oven to 190°C/gas 5.

2. Make the spice mix: put all the spices into a dry frying pan and roast until fragrant. Grind to a fine powder in a spice grinder or with a mortar and pestle.

3. Next make the tomato sauce. Heat 1 tablespoon of the coconut oil in a pan over a medium heat, then add the shallots, 1 of the cloves of garlic, the ginger and chopped coriander stalks. Add 1 tablespoon of the spice mixture and stir for 5 minutes (store the rest in an airtight container for up to 6 months). Add the chopped tomatoes and maple syrup. Cook for 10–15 minutes, then set aside. This will be the top layer of your dish.

4. Heat the remaining coconut oil in a separate pan and add the rest of the sliced garlic. When it is lightly golden, add the aubergine, okra and turmeric. Cook over a medium heat, stirring frequently, for 5–8 minutes. Once the vegetables have cooked down, add the spinach and immediately take off the heat. Divide this mixture between two ovenproof ramekins or pour into a large ovenproof dish, and then spoon the tomato sauce on top. Use the back of a spoon to make four little wells and then crack an egg into each one. Bake in the oven for about 10 minutes, or until done to your liking.

5. While the eggs are in the oven, make the dressing by combining the yoghurt with the lime zest and juice, a pinch of the spice mix, the red onion and a pinch of salt.

6. Now for the spicy oil: we like making it with butter but you can use oil. Simply heat together the butter and chilli flakes in a pan over a medium heat – take it off when it starts to brown a little.

7. When done, remove the eggs from the oven. To serve, dollop some of the yoghurt dressing on top and pour over the sizzling butter. Garnish with the coriander leaves, chilli and lime quarters and serve with hot naans or fresh flatbreads.

Tarragon, Ricotta and Parmesan Dippy Eggs

This is a wonderfully light yet indulgent baked egg. By whisking the egg whites it becomes more of a soufflé, really. We often have problems when making baked eggs – you want the yolk runny and the whites cooked, but we always seem to end up with hard yolks and runny whites, which is really disappointing after you have gone to the whole effort of a special breakfast. This recipe gives you a guaranteed runny yolk! We like to treat it more like a dippy egg, dunking in buttery sourdough soldiers.

Serves 4

4 eggs
a little flavourless oil
knob of butter
2 leeks, finely chopped
2 cloves garlic, finely chopped
1 red chilli, deseeded and
    finely chopped
2 teaspoons Dijon mustard
bunch of tarragon, woody
    stalks removed, leaves
    roughly chopped
200g ricotta
50g Parmesan, grated
salt and pepper
buttery toast soldiers, to serve

1. Preheat the oven to 200°C/gas 6.

2. Separate the eggs – put the whites into a medium bowl and the yolks onto a lightly oiled plate (this is to stop them sticking as you will need them later). Be careful not to pop the yolks.

3. Put the butter into a pan and melt over a medium heat. Add the leeks, garlic and chilli and fry for a few minutes until starting to caramelise. Take off the heat and stir in the mustard, tarragon, ricotta, half the Parmesan and seasoning.

4. Whisk the egg whites until soft peaks form, then carefully fold in the ricotta mixture, using a metal spoon.

5. Place four ramekins in front of you and divide some of the mixture between them, to come about two-thirds of the way up the ramekin. Then carefully place one egg yolk on top of the mixture. Very carefully spoon the remaining mixture on top of each yolk and sprinkle over the remaining Parmesan.

6. Put the ramekins onto a baking tray and bake in the oven for about 10 minutes, or until puffed up and brown on top with the yolk still runny. Serve immediately with buttery toast soldiers.

Quinoa and a Poached Egg
with Avocado, Peas and Crispy Kale

Serves 4

50g flaked almonds

50g cashew nuts

50g pine nuts

150g quinoa, washed and drained

4 large handfuls of kale,
tough stems removed,
roughly chopped

drizzle of olive oil

200g frozen peas

100g frozen edamame

bunch of sugar snap peas, sliced

bunch of spring onions, chopped

1 avocado, stone removed,
peeled and chopped

bunch of dill, chopped

bunch of coriander, chopped

splash of white wine vinegar

4 eggs

handful of pea shoots

1 red chilli, sliced

salt and pepper

FOR THE DRESSING

40ml olive oil

juice of 1 lemon

little squeeze of honey

1 teaspoon ground coriander

NICE ADDITIONS

200g broad beans

small bunch of asparagus,
blanched and sliced

2 courgettes, cut into squares
and roasted with olive oil,
salt and pepper

150g feta or goat's cheese,
crumbled

1 tablespoon harissa (or use our
Smoky Harissa – see page 259)

Jalapeño, Cashew and
Avocado Dip (see page 256;
it's exceptional with this)

100g pomegranate seeds

bunch of mint, leaves shredded

100g dried cranberries

A healthy, versatile breakfast dish. We always cook extra as it makes a very good lunch or dinner dish as well, perhaps with added chicken or some steamed fish. We first came up with the recipe when we had our pop-up restaurant in Queen's Park, London; breakfast and brunch were a big deal there and this was a permanent feature on the weekly changing menu. However, we would always tweak it to keep it exciting and different for those who ordered it daily. This recipe is just a suggestion, but there is no end to what you could add.

1. Preheat the oven to 220°C/gas 7. Put the almonds, cashew nuts and pine nuts on a baking tray, place in the oven and roast for 5–10 minutes until nicely golden. Cool and roughly chop.

2. Meanwhile, bring a pan of salted water to the boil. Add the quinoa and cook for about 15 minutes, until tender. Drain and cool under cold running water to stop it from overcooking, then drain thoroughly and add to a mixing bowl with the chopped nuts.

3. Put the kale on a baking tray, drizzle with olive oil and season with salt and pepper. Place in the oven for about 5 minutes until nicely crisp. Add to the quinoa bowl.

4. Pour boiling water over the peas and edamame to defrost; drain and add to the quinoa along with the sugar snaps, spring onions, avocado, dill and coriander. Whisk all the dressing ingredients together, pour over the mixture and stir to combine. Taste and season.

5. Poach the eggs: bring a pan of water to the boil then turn down to a simmer and add a splash of white wine vinegar. Crack an egg into a teacup, bring it close to the water and carefully tip the egg in. Bring the heat back up to a low boil so the bubbles help to push the white of the egg upwards – you can also use a spoon to help with this. Cook for 4–5 minutes, then remove from the pan and place in a bowl of cold water. Repeat for the rest of the eggs – you should be able to get a few eggs in the pan at one time.

6. Spoon the quinoa into bowls and top with the pea shoots. Place a poached egg on top of each bowl and sprinkle with the sliced red chilli.

Celeriac and Smoked Ham Rösti
with a Poached Egg and Lemon Crème Fraîche

Celeriac is often overlooked in the kitchen – maybe due to its alien appearance – but this shouldn't be the case. It is delicious, both raw and cooked, taking on different flavours and textures. This is the type of dish we would serve for a crowd-pleasing brunch at the weekend.

Serves 6–8

½ celeriac (approx. 300g), peeled and cut into 5cm chucks

knob of butter

2 tablespoons olive oil, plus extra if needed

1 leek, thinly sliced

2 cloves garlic, crushed

pinch of fresh thyme leaves

½ teaspoon chilli flakes

60g smoked ham, roughly cut or torn

60g Gruyère, grated

1 tablespoon Dijon mustard

pinch of finely chopped tarragon leaves

2 lemons, zested

1 egg, beaten

salt and pepper

FOR THE CRÈME FRAÎCHE DRESSING

1 tablespoon chopped tarragon leaves

5 tablespoons crème fraîche

1 lemon, zest and juice

TO SERVE

1–2 eggs per person

rocket or salad leaves of your choice

chopped red chilli (optional)

1. Bring a pan of water to the boil, add the celeriac and boil for 20 minutes until tender. Drain thoroughly and then mash, but not too smooth – it's nice to keep it a little lumpy.

2. Meanwhile, make the dressing by whisking together all the ingredients in a bowl. Set aside.

3. Add the butter and 1 tablespoon of the olive oil to a frying pan over a medium heat and stir-fry the leek with the garlic, thyme and chilli flakes. Once the leek is soft, after about 5 minutes, add the ham and cook for a further few minutes.

4. Add to a bowl with the grated cheese, mustard and tarragon. Mix in the celeriac and lemon zest and season to taste. Finally add the egg and mix in. Put in the fridge for at least 10 minutes to cool and set.

5. Poach the eggs (see opposite page) and set to one side (fried eggs are good with this, too).

6. Heat the remaining tablespoon of oil in a pan over a medium–high heat. Take the celeriac mixture out of the fridge and form into patties. Place the patties, a few at a time, in the hot pan and cook for a good few minutes on each side, until crisp and golden. Drain on kitchen paper while you cook the rest, adding more oil if needed.

7. Arrange a handful of rocket (or your choice of leaves) on a plate and add the rösti. Top with the poached eggs and drizzle the dressing over the top. We like adding some chopped chilli, too.

Mexican Green Eggs

This was created after a trip to New York in the spring, a favourite time to visit as the blossom is blooming and the pavements start to fill up with people eating outside. Breakfasts are always so inspiring there, especially when it comes to brunch. This is a fun little dish, vibrantly green in colour, with the added beautiful orange yolk that bursts into it. You could serve it in one big pan to feed the masses, or, if you serve it individually like we do here, we recommend using small cast-iron dishes or terracotta ramekins that can take a high heat beneath.

The tomatillos really make the dish here, and they're usually not too difficult to find; you can buy them in tins from most large supermarkets in the Mexican section, or you can buy them online.

Serves 4

FOR THE GREEN SAUCE
1 tablespoon olive oil, plus extra
  for the dish(es)
1 onion, finely chopped
3 cloves garlic, thickly sliced
1 teaspoon ground cumin
1 teaspoon ground coriander
1 x 300g tin tomatillos, drained
1 tablespoon hot sauce
1–2 teaspoons maple syrup
juice of ½ lemon
medium bunch of coriander
  (approx. 30g), leaves and stalks

TO SERVE
8 eggs
50g feta, crumbled
2 spring onions, thinly sliced
good pinch of chopped
  parsley leaves
toasted brioche or other toast

1. Heat the olive oil in a pan over a medium heat and sauté the chopped onion for a few minutes, then add the garlic. Cook for a few minutes until starting to turn translucent. Add the ground cumin and coriander, cook for a few more minutes and then take off the heat.

2. Pour the drained tomatillos into a blender along with the remaining ingredients, including the cooked onion mixture. Blitz until smooth.

3. Oil a large flameproof dish (or four individual dishes) and place over a low heat (you will probably have to cook these one by one if you are using individual dishes). Crack 2 eggs into each dish. Allow the eggs to cook sunny side up until the whites are fully cooked and the yolks are still runny. At this point, liberally spoon the sauce on top to cover the whites, leaving the yolks poking out. Crumble over a little feta and sprinkle the spring onions and parsley on top. Serve with toast – we recommend griddled brioche with this.

Turkish Poached Eggs
with Sage and Chilli Butter

Although this dish is not bad for you, it is rich and rather luxurious. It's just right for a Saturday morning when you feel like spoiling yourself – you almost feel like it should be eaten while wearing cashmere and soft, expensive slippers.

This recipe is a take on the Turkish dish *çılbır*, and features a dense garlicky yoghurt swirled into spicy butter with richness from the egg yolks running through, just waiting to be mopped up with crusty bread. The dish is known as a Turkish comfort food and originates from the Ottoman Empire – it has stuck around so long for good reason!

Serves 2

FOR THE GARLIC YOGHURT
150g natural yoghurt
1 clove garlic, crushed
1 teaspoon ground cumin
salt and pepper

FOR THE SPINACH
splash of olive oil
3 spring onions, chopped
200g spinach
pinch of ground nutmeg

FOR THE CHILLI BUTTER
30g salted butter
1 teaspoon chilli flakes
small bunch of sage leaves, chopped

TO SERVE
2–4 eggs, to taste (see page 38)
handful of toasted pine nuts
sliced spring onions, sliced red chilli, coriander leaves, chopped dill or a pinch of sumac, to garnish
sourdough toast or warm flatbreads

1. First make the yoghurt by whisking all the ingredients together and seasoning to taste. Leave to one side, but not in the fridge – you want to serve it at room temperature.

2. Next make the spinach. Heat the olive oil in a pan and add the chopped spring onions. Sauté for a couple of minutes then add the spinach and stir so it starts to wilt. Add the nutmeg and season with salt and pepper. Once wilted, cover to keep warm.

3. Now make the butter: melt the butter in a pan until starting to foam, then add the chilli flakes and the sage leaves so they sizzle. Cook for another 30 seconds then take off the heat.

4. Poach the eggs to your liking (see page 38).

5. Divide the spinach mixture between warmed plates, then add the yoghurt, then the poached eggs. Spoon the hot butter over the top and finish with a handful of toasted pine nuts and any other desired garnishes. Serve with sourdough toast or warm flatbreads.

This is a fun one to make into a breakfast bruschetta – lay a flatbread or piece of toasted sourdough down, drizzle with olive oil. Layer up the spinach, yoghurt, egg and chilli butter – a fried egg would be good here too, if you prefer.

Spring Green Bruschetta
with Tart's Scrambled Eggs

Bruschetta features a lot in our cooking, and we have come to use the term loosely – to us it's really a fancy word for something on toast, in most cases sourdough – although we know this relaxed approach might annoy Italian purists slightly! The bruschetta is a handy one though: it's great for a snack or a canapé, but also (as in this case) a meal in itself (see pages 66–71 for more fun bruschetta ideas). This is a quick and easy number when something slightly more substantial is wanted for your breakfast. When it comes to the greens, use what you like – we love adding wild garlic when it is in season. But really it is all about the eggs – this is our absolute favourite way of doing scrambled.

Makes 2 large bruschetta

FOR THE GREENS

1 teaspoon olive oil, plus extra for drizzling

8 spring onions, roots and leafy ends trimmed (but otherwise kept whole)

2 cloves garlic, crushed (or use a small bunch of wild garlic)

large bunch of rainbow chard

4 big handfuls of spinach

salt and pepper

FOR THE EGGS

knob of butter

4 spring onions, chopped

1 red chilli, deseeded and finely chopped

4 eggs, beaten

2 teaspoons Dijon mustard

small bunch of basil, leaves chopped

small bunch of coriander, leaves chopped

2 handfuls of grated cheese (optional)

TO SERVE

2 slices of sourdough or bread of your choice, toasted

harissa, to taste (or use our Smoky Harissa – see page 259)

1. First prepare the greens: heat the olive oil in a small pan over a medium heat, add the spring onions and leave to sizzle for a few minutes before adding the garlic and sautéing for 2 minutes. Add the chard and spinach and wilt down, then season with salt and pepper and keep warm while you toast your bread.

2. Once the bread is toasted, drizzle with oil and top with the greens.

3. Now for the eggs: heat the butter in a frying pan, add the spring onions and chilli and cook for a couple of minutes, then add the eggs, Dijon mustard and a pinch of salt and pepper and cook for a couple of minutes, using a rubber spatula to keep the eggs moving in the pan. Quickly add the herbs and cheese (if using), combine with the eggs, then tip straight out of the pan onto the greens – if you leave it in the pan it will carry on cooking and go hard. This is very good topped with a spoonful of our Smoky Harissa sauce (see page 259).

Spiced Sweet Potato Pancakes
with Avocado Salsa

This is an old Tart classic, which we created when we opened our first pop-up restaurant, Tart's Kitchen, in Queen's Park, London. We found an amazing space, which was an old brewery with huge windows and lovely old exposed brick – but with no kitchen, so we had to build the whole thing! We had a lot of fun, it was the perfect party venue. We changed the menu from week to week and at the weekends it was all-day brunch. The weekend brunch was the highlight, with queues around the corner, windows flung open and people lounging in the sun. We loved it.

Serves 4

FOR THE PANCAKES

1 sweet potato (approx. 500g), peeled and cut into cubes

1 tablespoon coconut oil

3 spring onions, finely chopped

1 clove garlic, crushed

small bunch of coriander, stalks and leaves chopped

1 green chilli, deseeded and finely chopped

2 limes, zested

2 teaspoons garam masala

1 egg, beaten

2 tablespoons flour (gluten-free flour would work here)

1 teaspoon baking powder

big pinch of grated Cheddar or crumbled goat's cheese (optional)

splash of olive oil

salt and pepper

FOR THE AVOCADO SALSA

1 avocado, stone removed, peeled and cut into small cubes

handful of sweet tomatoes, finely chopped

1 spring onion, finely chopped

1 clove garlic, crushed

1 red chilli, deseeded and finely chopped

small bunch of chopped coriander

1 teaspoon ground cumin

juice of ½ lime

a little olive oil

salt and pepper

TO SERVE

4 poached eggs (see page 38)

mixed salad leaves

lime wedges

1. Bring a large pan of water to the boil and cook the sweet potato for about 20 minutes. Test to see if it is cooked by prodding with a knife; it should slide in easily. Drain, then lightly mash with the coconut oil and season with salt and pepper. Mix through the remaining ingredients except the olive oil and set aside.

2. In a bowl, mix together the avocado salsa ingredients, reserving a little of the chopped chilli and a few coriander leaves to garnish. Season well with salt and pepper.

3. Poach your eggs to your liking (see page 38) – although this would also be good with fried eggs.

4. Heat a large non-stick pan over a medium heat and add a drizzle of olive oil. Drop tablespoons of the pancake mixture into the pan (flatten a little with the bottom of the spoon) and fry until nicely golden on each side. Repeat until the mixture is used up (you should get about 8 pancakes).

5. Serve hot with a poached egg on top and the salsa spooned on the side. Garnish with chopped chillies and coriander leaves. We like to add a few salad leaves and a squeeze of lime too – and it would also be delicious with a really good Bloody Mary.

Banana and Oat Pancakes
with Peanut Cream and Roast Bananas

Grains ground to flour, mixed with milk and eggs and cooked in a pan to form little cakes are some of the earliest foods known to mankind. You can tweak this simple base by adding different ground grains or nuts, fruit, sweeteners and milks. We are big fans of using buttermilk – it makes a fluffier pancake, the acidity kick-starting the bicarbonate of soda – but we also love it for its delicious subtle tang. We are also huge fans of banana pancakes – they are so moist and indulgent. Pancakes are the perfect vehicle for adding lots of toppings too, which is always – even in adulthood – very exciting…

Serves 6

5 ripe bananas

100g crunchy peanut butter

100g mascarpone

2 eggs

200ml buttermilk

1 teaspoon vanilla extract

50ml maple syrup

pinch of sea salt

75g rolled oats, blitzed in a food processor until finely ground

75g self-raising flour

1 teaspoon bicarbonate of soda

1 heaped tablespoon of coconut oil, melted, plus 1–2 tablespoons extra, for frying (optional)

1–2 tablespoons groundnut oil, for frying (optional)

fresh blueberries and raspberries, to serve (optional)

1. First make the roast bananas. Preheat the oven to 220°C/gas 7. Slice 3 of the bananas lengthways, place them on a baking tray covered with foil (to cut down on washing-up) and stick in the oven for about 15 minutes until starting to caramelise. Remove from the oven.

2. Now make the peanut cream: simply beat the crunchy peanut butter and mascarpone together, then set aside.

3. To make the pancakes, mash the remaining 2 bananas with a fork in a mixing bowl – don't worry about making them completely smooth, they can be a little rough. In a separate bowl whisk together the eggs, buttermilk, vanilla extract, maple syrup and sea salt before adding the mashed bananas.

4. Combine the ground oats, flour and baking powder and fold into the wet ingredients, being careful not to overmix. Stir the heaped tablespoon of melted coconut oil into the mixture and let it sit for a couple of minutes

5. Next place a frying pan over a medium heat and drizzle in a little groundnut or coconut oil. Dollop 2 tablespoons of mixture into the pan for each pancake and spread into an even circle. Cook for about 3 minutes each side – wait for bubbles to appear all over the surface before flipping and cooking the other side. The cooked side should be golden brown. Repeat with the remaining batter, adding more oil to the pan as needed.

6. Serve the pancakes hot with the roasted bananas on the side and a dollop of the peanut cream. We also like to add a few fresh berries and extra maple syrup on top.

Pumpkin, Cinnamon and Pecan Muffins
with Maple Butter

These remind us of the bakeries in Toronto, where Jemima was born. Just the smell of the little golden muffins cooking makes us want to cancel our day's plans and get tucked into bed with cups of tea, a good TV series and a couple of these muffins, warm from the oven and slathered with salty maple butter.

You could also substitute the pumpkin for sweet potato, or use an alternative flour – we like white spelt flour as it gives the muffins a nutty depth.

Makes 6

200g pumpkin, cut into 5cm chunks and seeds scraped out
100g butter
120g brown sugar, plus a pinch for the tops
2 eggs
1 teaspoon vanilla extract
200g white spelt flour
1 teaspoon bicarbonate of soda
1 teaspoon baking powder
1 teaspoon grated nutmeg
1 teaspoon ground cinnamon
1 teaspoon ground ginger
1 teaspoon sea salt
50g chopped pecans (reserve a pinch for the tops)
generous pinch of porridge oats
a sprinkle of oats for the top

FOR THE MAPLE BUTTER
100g butter, at room temperature
2 tablespoons maple syrup
1 teaspoon ground cinnamon
pinch of sea salt

1. Preheat the oven to 200°C/gas 6 and line a baking tray with baking paper. Line a 6-hole muffin tray with paper cases.

2. First make the maple butter. Beat the butter in a bowl with a wooden spoon until soft and creamy. Then add the maple syrup, cinnamon and salt and beat until combined. Turn out onto a big piece of cling film, roll it around the butter to make a sausage shape, then twist the ends to seal. Place in the fridge to firm up.

3. Place the cut pumpkin pieces on the baking tray, sprinkle with a little water and bake for 20 minutes until cooked through and soft (check by poking it with a knife). Remove from the oven and reduce the temperature to 190°C/gas 5. Scrape the flesh away from the skins with a spoon and then mash with a masher or fork until smooth.

4. Whisk together the butter and sugar until fluffy, then add the eggs one at a time, followed by the vanilla extract, then the pumpkin purée.

5. In a separate bowl, mix together the flour, bicarbonate of soda, baking powder, spices, sea salt and chopped pecans. When combined, fold the dry ingredients into the pumpkin mixture.

6. Use a spoon to fill the muffin cases to the top with the mixture. Mix the oats with the reserved pecans and brown sugar, then sprinkle over the muffins. Bake for 20–25 minutes.

7. Serve the muffins warm with slices of maple butter to spread on.

Small Plates

Nothing is quite so enticing as a table full of lots of delicious small plates.

This is when food has the most impact – lots of small bold plates with all the extra zing, crunch, oozy-ness, spice and sizzle you could hope for. It's when cooking gets exciting and inventive – nothing is quite so enticing as a table full of lots of delicious small plates. We usually find ourselves sharing lots of starters in restaurants, trying as many different tastes and textures as we can and enjoying the variety of colours and harmonious flavours. We love this style of eating, when you can be your own boss and get carried away with indulging yourself, tasting as little or as much of each thing as takes your fancy.

This chapter can either be used for fun dishes to share with your friends and for good party nibbles like our Sweet Potato and Chorizo Croquetas or Smoky Taramasalata, or for individual tasty little starters and even elegant lunch dishes, like our Sea Bass Carpaccio or Baby Squid, Fennel and Black Ink. We particularly like this style of eating for al fresco dining – we are lucky enough to both live near parks in London, so on sunny days we often find ourselves packing baskets with blankets and delicious little bites, or sitting out in our little gardens feasting on Flatbread Pizzas and Truffle Polenta Balls.

They are all wonderfully simple to prepare, taking away the fear of the laborious fiddly starter or time-consuming party food spread. And they all go very well with a glass of good wine and some great company.

Smoky Taramasalata

Artichoke Dip

Smoked Prawns with Aioli

Sea Bass Carpaccio

Truffle Polenta Balls

Tuna Tostadas

Bruschetta

Crab Gratin

Baby Squid, Fennel and Black Ink

Sweet Potato and Chorizo Croquetas

Easy Chicken and Pickled Ginger Gyozas

Saffron Roasted Peppers

Fish Tacos

Roasted Cauliflower, Feta and Coriander Frittata

Middle Eastern Spiced Aubergine Gratins

Sticky Miso Spare Ribs

Flatbread Pizzas

Roast Tomato and Harissa Tart

Smoky Taramasalata

This is a delicious little twist on the classic tarama. The smoked salmon adds a lovely, complementary smoky flavour.

Cod's roe is easy to buy from your local fishmonger; and do try and get a good reputable smoked salmon that has been smoked in a sustainable way, without using dye – you will really taste the difference. The Secret Smokehouse, set up independently in east London, is excellent and we highly recommend it for smoked fish, especially haddock, salmon, trout and kippers.

Serves 4–6

100g crustless sourdough bread
200g cod's roe
120g smoked salmon
1 lemon, zest and juice
1 shallot, finely chopped
1 large clove garlic, crushed
2 teaspoons Dijon mustard
200ml light olive oil
salt and pepper

1. Soak the bread in a small bowl of water for 5 minutes, then remove and squeeze to get rid of any excess water.
2. Put the bread in a food processor, add all the remaining ingredients except the olive oil and seasoning, and blitz until smooth.
3. With the motor running, slowly pour the olive oil into the machine in a steady stream until combined. Season to taste and serve with toast or crudités.

Artichoke Dip

We first had artichoke dip in New York at a restaurant in the Lower East Side called Freemans, a very low-key place hidden down an alley. Inside was very 'rustic-luxe', with wooden tables, antlers on the walls, candles and hot waiters in checked shirts serving really good red wine. Very cool. We would order the artichoke dip, a huge pot of mussels and an enormous plate of bread, along with the cheapest wine on the menu. What more could you want in life?

Here is our devilish version, a favourite of Lucy's sister Hannah, who dreams about the stuff.

Serves 4–6

splash of olive oil or knob
  of butter
1 leek, roughly chopped
2 cloves garlic, roughly chopped
1 sprig of rosemary, leaves
  stripped
200g tinned artichoke
  hearts, drained
2 tablespoons mayonnaise
2 tablespoons crème fraîche
1 teaspoon Dijon mustard
1–2 teaspoons cayenne pepper,
  or to taste
juice of ½ lemon
150g smoked Cheddar, grated
salt and pepper
2 tablespoons grated Parmesan,
  for the topping
toasted sourdough, to serve

1. Preheat the oven to 220°C/gas 7.
2. Heat the olive oil or butter in a frying pan and lightly sauté the leek, garlic and rosemary until softened, then remove and transfer to a food processor.
3. Add the rest of the ingredients except for the Parmesan (and go easy when seasoning with the salt). Pulse until blended, but still chunky. Transfer to an ovenproof dish and sprinkle over the Parmesan. Bake in the oven for 10–12 minutes until golden and bubbling on the top. Serve with toasted sourdough.

Smoked Prawns with Lemon Aioli

Up in Northumberland, in a seaside town called Seahouses, they have a well-known fishmonger with a properly good smokehouse. We bought a bag of smoked prawns from them and decided to try one in the car; before we knew it we had polished off the lot and made a huge mess with shells all over the place. We have dreamed about them ever since and, when getting into our smoking obsession, thought we must give them a try. They are so easy and my God are they good – a marriage made in heaven when smoked with alder woodchips. They are great as a starter, or make a nice canapé if your guests don't mind getting their fingers messy – not for a precious crowd.

1. Set up the smoker following the instructions on page 271, using the alder woodchips.
2. When you start to see wisps of smoke coming out of the smoker, add the prawns and close the lid. Cook for 10–15 minutes, depending on size, over a low heat. They should be blushing pink and cooked through. Once done, take off the heat and leave to cool.
3. Make the aioli: put the egg yolk, garlic, mustard, lemon juice, salt and pepper into a bowl and whisk together. Mix the two oils together in a jug and very slowly add these to the egg yolk mixture, whisking all the time and making sure the oil has been fully incorporated before adding more. Continue until the sauce has emulsified and thickened. Taste and add a little more seasoning if needed.
4. Serve the smoked prawns with the lemon aioli, and lots of napkins.

Serves 4–5

8–10 raw prawns, shell on
2 tablespoons alder woodchips, soaked in water for 2 minutes

FOR THE AIOLI
1 egg yolk
1 clove garlic, crushed
½ teaspoon Dijon mustard
juice of ½ lemon
100ml groundnut oil
100ml extra virgin olive oil
salt and pepper

Sea Bass Carpaccio
with Oregano, Tomato and Olive Oil

Sometimes the simplest recipes are hard to beat – especially when you use the best-quality ingredients. This is a pretty fantastic dish served as a dinner party starter. The only hitch is that it has to be sliced and dressed at the last minute as the lemon will quickly 'cook' the fish. Serve on a big serving plate or individual plates, with warm crusty bread.

It is very important to use good-quality olive oil in this recipe – not your everyday supermarket number – and we like to use a peppery Italian one. Good olive oil does not come cheap so once you have bought a bottle, store it in a cool dark cupboard and bring it out for occasions like this.

1. Place the fish on a board and check it carefully for any stray bones; use pliers or tweezers to remove any that are left. Slice the flesh against the grain into thin slices, supporting the fillet with your free hand. For this you will need a sharp, flexible filleting knife. Starting at the centre of a large plate, arrange the thin slices of sea bass slightly overlapping each other and moving radially outwards until the plate is covered.

2. Drizzle over the lemon juice and olive oil – don't overdo the lemon juice as the tomatoes also have acidity.

3. Scatter over the chopped tomato, chilli and oregano. Sprinkle with sea salt, garnish with radishes and edible flowers, if using, and serve at once.

Serves 4–6

500g sushi-grade skinless wild sea bass fillet

juice of 1 lemon

4 tablespoons extra virgin olive oil

6–8 (approx.) cherry tomatoes, deseeded and very finely chopped

1 large red chilli, deseeded and very finely chopped

pinch of very finely chopped fresh oregano leaves

sliced radishes and edible flowers, for garnish (optional)

sea salt

Truffle Polenta Balls

These little crispy hot mouthfuls are indulgent, salty and gooey and the truffle adds a touch of sophistication. This is the sort of thing we like to serve at a drinks party – you have to love something hot and cheesy! When it comes to canapés we like a delicious bruschetta, chunks of very good cheese or ham, delicate sweet anchovies or some wonderful Italian olives, and something hot and crispy like this. We are not so much into itty bitty posh canapés – it's a bore and the last thing you want to eat is a mouthful of cold risotto served on a spoon. It is all about keeping it simple and using very good-quality ingredients.

Serves 8–10

750ml stock (or water)

150g quick-cook polenta, plus extra for coating the balls (about 50g)

2 tablespoons finely grated Parmesan

2 lemons, zested

3–4 sprigs of rosemary, leaves stripped and chopped

1–2 tablespoons truffle oil

1 clove garlic, crushed

100g taleggio, cut into 1cm chunks

2 eggs

olive oil or groundnut oil, for frying

salt and pepper

1. Bring the stock or water to the boil and then reduce the heat to a simmer. Pour the polenta in steadily, stirring constantly with a wooden spoon. Continue to stir until the polenta has thickened and starts to come away from the sides of the pan. Stir in the Parmesan, lemon zest, half of the chopped rosemary, the truffle oil and the crushed garlic. Season well.

2. Pour the polenta into a bowl, cover and place in the fridge until cool (about 20 minutes).

3. When cool, remove from the fridge. Take around 1 tablespoon of the mixture, flatten it into a thin-ish pancake in your palm and place a chunk of taleggio into the middle. Wrap the mixture around the cheese. Repeat with the rest of the polenta mixture and cheese chunks.

4. Beat the eggs in a bowl. Place the remaining chopped rosemary on a small plate with plenty of sea salt and the extra dry polenta. Drop a polenta ball into the egg mixture, then roll it in the dry mixture. Repeat until all the balls are coated.

5. Heat enough oil to shallow-fry your balls in a frying pan. Fry in batches over a medium-high heat until golden brown on all sides, about 5 minutes. Blot off excess oil on kitchen paper and serve immediately.

Tuna Tostadas
with Mango, Crispy Corn and Jalapeño Sauce

This is a very pretty, light and fresh tostada that is both juicy and zingy – the sweet mango and the spicy jalapeño gives it just the right balance. If you can't find ready-made tostadas, you can use soft tortillas and either bake, fry or grill them until crisp. Use biscuit cutters to cut out small tostadas if you have big tortillas.

Makes 4–6 small tostadas

200g sushi-grade tuna

2 tablespoons shop-bought roasted and salted corn kernels

½ mango, peeled and cut into small squares

small bunch of coriander, leaves chopped

small bunch of mint, leaves chopped

½ large red chilli, deseeded and finely chopped

¼ red onion, thinly sliced

juice and zest of 2 limes

4 tortillas (or shop-bought tostadas)

1–2 avocados (depending on size), stone removed, peeled and thinly sliced

2 tablespoons very good extra virgin olive oil, plus extra for frying the tortillas

FOR THE JALAPEÑO, LIME AND GINGER SAUCE

3 tinned jalapeños (or about 8 slices from a jar), drained

½ shallot, peeled

small bunch of coriander

5cm piece of fresh ginger, peeled

1 tablespoon honey

juice of 1 lime

salt and pepper

1. First make the sauce: blitz all the ingredients together in a food processor or blender. Check the seasoning and set aside.

2. Carefully chop the tuna into small dice and put in a bowl. Add the corn, mango, coriander, mint, chilli, red onion and lime zest and toss together.

3. Now make your tostadas: cut the tortillas into rounds using a biscuit cutter or a knife. Heat a little oil in a frying pan over a medium heat and lightly fry the tortillas on both sides until crisp. Transfer to kitchen paper and dab to remove excess oil.

4. Place the tostadas on a plate, then lay a few slices of avocado on each.

5. Drizzle the olive oil over the tuna mix, season and squeeze over the lime juice. Carefully combine, then divide between the tostadas. Drizzle over the jalapeño sauce and serve. It is equally delicious with the Jalapeño, Cashew and Avocado Dip on page 256.

Bruschetta

The word bruschetta comes from the Latin verb *bruscare* – to char or toast. They are traditionally an antipasto: simply charred bread drizzled with olive oil and rubbed with a clove of garlic. For us they bring back memories of summer evenings in Tuscany, with mums griddling sliced sourdough on the barbecue and the irresistible smells of torn basil, sweet tomatoes and garlic – this simple combination is still for us the ultimate bruschetta, fresh and juicy with a little *piccante* heat.

These delicious open-style sandwiches have now been transformed into countless easy dishes to supplement your lunches or pre-dinner nibbles. Seemingly simple bruschetta that use great-quality ingredients are usually the winners; they can also save you in a time of need (such as starvation at lunch time!). We love to shop for quick-to-assemble bruschetta ingredients at Giacobazzi in north London, a great Italian deli. We highly recommend a visit there. They stock delicious sourdoughs, cheese, fresh pasta, sliced cured meats, olive oils and many more fantastic delights.

Each recipe here makes 2 large or 4–6 small bruschetta.

Slow-cooked Courgette with Mint, Chilli and Ricotta

2 courgettes

splash of extra virgin olive oil, plus extra for drizzling

1 small red chilli, finely chopped (leave the seeds if you want it hot)

1 lemon, zested, plus a squeeze of juice

small bunch of mint, leaves finely chopped

toasted sourdough slices

1 clove garlic, halved

250g ricotta

sea salt

1. Slice the courgettes on a mandoline crossways as thinly as possible, or slice very thinly with a knife.

2. Heat a frying pan with a splash of olive oil, add the sliced courgettes and chopped chilli. Slow cook for around 20 minutes, stirring every few minutes. Add the lemon zest, a little squeeze of lemon juice, the mint (reserving a little to garnish) and some sea salt.

3. Rub each griddled piece of toast with the cut side of the garlic and drizzle with a little extra virgin olive oil. Smother generously with the ricotta, spreading to the edges, then top with the courgettes and garnish with a little more mint. These go very well with a cold glass of Chardonnay.

Roasted Figs with Strained Yoghurt, Honeycomb, Truffle and Hazelnut

1. Line a sieve with two squares of cheesecloth and spoon the yoghurt into the middle. Pull the corners together and twist, squeezing out the liquid. Leave in the sieve in a cool place (over the sink or a bowl) to drain for 1–2 hours.

2. Preheat the oven to 200°C/gas 6 and line a baking tray with baking paper. Cut the figs in half, place on the lined tray and roast for about 20 minutes until golden and bubbling. Remove from the oven and set aside to cool.

3. When you come to use the yoghurt, give the bundle a really good squeeze, letting out as much liquid as you can before the yoghurt starts to seep out. Open up the cheesecloth bundle and scrape out the yoghurt.

4. Drizzle the griddled sourdough slices with extra virgin olive oil and lay on a board. Spoon over the strained yoghurt and dot over the roasted fig slices.

5. With a teaspoon, cut away at the honeycomb and dot around on top of the figs (or drizzle with a little honey). Sprinkle over the hazelnuts and finish with a drizzle of truffle oil (if you have actual truffles this is the time to use them – shave them over the top).

400g yoghurt

6 figs

toasted sourdough slices

drizzle of extra virgin olive oil

good chunk of honeycomb (or a squeeze of honey)

handful of toasted hazelnuts, roughly chopped

drizzle of truffle oil

drizzle of extra virgin olive oil

toasted sourdough slices

1 avocado, stone removed, peeled and sliced

2–3 smoked mackerel fillets (we like the ones with cracked black pepper)

1 red chilli, deseeded and finely chopped

juice of 1 lime

small handful of coriander leaves, chopped

salt and pepper

Mackerel, Lime and Chilli

1. Drizzle olive oil over the toasts, top with the avocado slices then break up the mackerel fillets and add these too.

2. Scatter with chopped chilli, squeeze over some lime juice and season to taste. Finish by scattering with coriander, then chop in half and eat!

Roast Garlic with Mozzarella, Tomato and Basil

1. Preheat the oven to 200°C/gas 6.
2. Chop off the top of the head of the garlic, just enough to slightly reveal the cloves, and place in an ovenproof dish, sprinkle with some water and put in the oven. Roast for about 30 minutes until the cloves are starting to bubble out of the top. Set aside to cool.
3. While the garlic is in the oven, place the tomatoes in a separate ovenproof dish, drizzle with olive oil, season with salt and pepper and place in the oven for 20–30 minutes until starting to colour.
4. Drizzle the sourdough toast with olive oil. Squeeze the garlic cloves out of their skins (messy business!) and spread onto the toast. Top with mozzarella, roasted tomatoes, basil, a drizzle more olive oil and some salt and pepper.

1 large head of garlic
handful of cherry tomatoes
drizzle of extra virgin olive oil
toasted sourdough slices
1 buffalo mozzarella ball, torn or sliced
small handful of basil leaves, roughly torn
salt and pepper

Another option for this bruschetta is to top the roasted garlic with a few fresh white anchovies – you want the nice plump, sweet fillets, not the salty hairy ones you get in tins.

White Bean and Parma Ham

1. Heat the olive oil in a pan over a medium heat and sauté the leek, shallot, garlic, chilli flakes and chopped herbs. Cook, stirring, for 3–5 minutes. Add the stock and simmer down a little, then add the beans; cook for a further few minutes.
2. Blitz in a food processor until you have a coarse paste. Season generously and add the lemon zest and a squeeze of lemon juice.
3. Heat a small frying pan and add a generous glug of olive oil. When the oil is very hot, add the extra sage leaves and fry for 30 seconds until just crisp, then remove to a piece of kitchen paper.
4. Heat a griddle pan until very hot, drizzle the sourdough toast with olive oil and place on the griddle pan until charred with lines on both sides. Remove from the heat and place on a board.
5. Generously spoon on the white beans, followed by a piece of Parma ham and a generous amount of chopped parsley. Add a few crispy sage leaves and another drizzle of extra virgin olive oil.

splash of olive oil, plus extra for frying and drizzling
1 leek, finely chopped
1 shallot, finely chopped
2 cloves garlic, finely chopped
½ teaspoon chilli flakes
1 sprig each of sage and rosemary, leaves stripped and finely chopped, plus extra sage leaves for frying
60ml chicken stock (or vegetable stock or water)
1 x 400g tin cannellini beans, drained
1 lemon, zested, plus juice of ½
4 toasted sourdough slices
4 slices of very good-quality Parma ham
handful of chopped parsley leaves
drizzle of extra virgin olive oil
salt and pepper

More Bruschetta Ideas

Gorgonzola, figs, crisped Parma ham, balsamic vinegar

———

Manchego, red onion marmalade, asparagus, truffle oil

———

Sweetest summer tomatoes, homemade basil pesto

———

Ricotta, peas, broad beans, mint, dill, lemon zest

———

Roasted fennel, Parma ham, basil, chilli

———

Crab, shaved fennel, chilli, lemon, parsley

Goat's cheese, roasted tomatoes, basil

———

Roasted peppers, ricotta, basil, chilli

———

Roast aubergine, red onion and tomato, aged balsamic vinegar, burrata, pine nuts, basil

———

Mushrooms, thyme, mozzarella, truffle oil

———

Cavolo nero, prosciutto, garlic, chilli

———

Smoked trout, crème fraîche, tarragon, lemon

Goat's cheese, roast grapes and thyme, truffle honey

———

Ripe tomatoes, red wine vinegar, garlic, olive oil, basil

———

Smashed broad beans and peas, buffalo mozzarella, rocket

———

Wild mushrooms, garlic, thyme, tarragon, poached egg

———

Borlotti beans, rosemary, garlic, oregano, chilli flakes, olive oil

———

Mascarpone, peanut butter, roast banana, honey

Crab Gratin
with a Fennel and Parmesan Crust

This is a good little starter – it feels quite indulgent, although it is actually on the lighter side. It often crops up when we are making last-minute dinner plans, because after picking up the crabmeat everything else is pretty much in the store cupboard. You can whip it up and a few minutes later it's bubbling away in the oven ready to be devoured with crispy bread and a bottle of white wine picked up from the corner shop.

1. Preheat the grill to high.
2. Heat the butter in a small pan over a medium heat and add the shallot, garlic and chilli flakes. Sauté for a couple of minutes until translucent, then pour in the white wine, stock and lemon zest and allow to bubble for a moment. Add the crab and season with salt and pepper, then take off the heat and pour the crab mixture into an ovenproof dish.
3. Mix the topping ingredients together, season well, then spoon lightly over the crab mixture. Place the dish under the grill for 5 minutes. Meanwhile, combine the crème fraîche with a squeeze of lemon juice and season with salt and pepper.
4. Remove the gratin from the grill, dollop on the crème fraîche, sprinkle with the parsley and dig in. Serve with good white wine.

Serves 1–2

small knob of butter

1 banana shallot, very finely chopped

1 clove garlic, crushed

small pinch of chilli flakes

1 tablespoon white wine

4 tablespoons stock (vegetable, chicken or fish)

½ lemon, zested, plus a squeeze of juice

150g white and brown crabmeat, mixed

1 tablespoon crème fraîche

few sprigs of parsley, leaves chopped

salt and pepper

FOR THE TOPPING

1 tablespoon dried breadcrumbs

1 tablespoon grated Parmesan

½ teaspoon fennel seeds

1 teaspoon olive oil

Baby Squid, Fennel
and Black Ink

Black squid ink is used in a wide variety of traditional recipes throughout Europe. The ink is rich in flavour, adding depth and a little sweetness to dishes. This recipe steps away from the classic Italian uses of risotto, pasta or polenta, keeping it simple with caramelised fennel, soft squid and a zing from chilli and lemon, which makes it a very sophisticated little starter. Served with the lights down low, twinkling candles and white tablecloths, it adds to the dramatic atmosphere.

1. Heat the olive oil in a large pan and sauté the onions, fennel, garlic, thyme and chilli flakes. Cook over a medium heat, stirring as you go and reducing the heat if anything starts to catch. You want it all to cook down and caramelise – this will take about 15 minutes.

2. Next, pour in the wine and stock and add the squid. Put the lid on and cook for 15–20 minutes. Add a little water if it starts to thicken into a sauce – you want a loose consistency.

3. Add the squid ink, a good squeeze of lemon juice, the butter, if using, and the chopped tarragon. Stir well until all is combined.

4. Serve hot in warmed shallow bowls with a dollop of crème fraîche and a good scattering of chopped parsley and chilli, if using.

Serves 6

glug of olive oil

2 onions, finely chopped

2 bulbs fennel, thinly sliced into half-moons

4 cloves garlic, finely chopped

small bunch of thyme, leaves stripped and finely chopped

1 teaspoon chilli flakes

1 large glass of white wine (approx. 250ml)

250ml stock (vegetable or chicken), or water

800g fresh baby squid (from a sustainable source), cleaned and bodies cut into rings

4 tablespoons squid ink

squeeze of lemon juice

2 tablespoons butter (optional)

small bunch tarragon, leaves chopped

TO SERVE

crème fraîche

bunch of parsley, leaves finely chopped

1 big chilli, sliced into thin rings (optional)

Sweet Potato and Chorizo Croquetas

We created this recipe for one of our first ever columns in the *Evening Standard* magazine. It has turned out to be one of the most popular recipes we have written, with people still making them now, which is always very nice to hear. They have come up in conversation in the funniest of places, from the hairdressers, to a shoe shop, to standing in a queue in the butchers. We are always very happy to hear they were such a hit.

Makes 15–20

2 medium sweet potatoes, peeled and cut into 3cm cubes

splash of olive oil, plus extra for drizzling

200g chorizo, cut into 1cm cubes

200g feta, crumbled

4 spring onions, finely chopped

2 cloves garlic, very finely chopped

small bunch of coriander, leaves finely chopped

2 green chillies, deseeded and finely chopped

2 eggs

2 tablespoons panko breadcrumbs, plus extra for coating

1 tablespoon ground cumin

1 tablespoon ground coriander

2 teaspoons smoked paprika

salt and pepper

1. Preheat the oven to 200°C/gas 6 and line a couple of baking trays with baking paper.

2. Bring a large pan of water to the boil and cook the sweet potato cubes until tender, about 15–20 minutes. Make sure they are cooked through, then mash (leaving the texture a little chunky) and set aside to cool.

3. While the potatoes are cooling, heat the olive oil in a small frying pan and fry the chorizo until crisp.

4. In a large bowl, combine the mashed sweet potato, feta, chorizo, spring onions, garlic, coriander, chillies, 1 beaten egg, panko breadcrumbs and spices. Chill in the fridge until cold and stiff.

5. When cool, form the mixture into ovals or rounds. Beat the remaining egg in a bowl, then scatter panko breadcrumbs on a plate and season. Dip the croquetas into the beaten egg and then roll in the breadcrumbs. Place the croquetas on the lined baking trays as you go.

6. To cook, drizzle the croquetas with olive oil and bake in the oven for 5–10 minutes, or until crisp. For extra crispiness, slide under a hot grill for a few minutes until golden brown. (You could also shallow-fry the croquetas in olive oil.) Serve with a spiced yoghurt dip (see page 257).

Easy Chicken and Pickled Ginger Gyozas

We visited the magnificent 'land of the rising sun' a few years ago – it completely blew us away. It was funny to realise how they see gyoza in the same way that we might see a hot dog or a kebab from a fast food joint. It's a huge difference to the trendy hype they have here!

Traditional gyozas are made with minced pork, but we use chicken – both are delicious but chicken feels a little lighter.

Gyoza wrappers are great to have in your freezer (they can be bought in any Asian supermarket, in the freezer section of some of the bigger supermarket chains and online). Once defrosted, they take minutes to fill and cook – instant all-round happiness. Put any unused wrappers back in the freezer for next time. You can make big batches of dumplings and then freeze them, too. When you fancy a dumpling fix, just cook them straight from frozen!

Makes about 20

1 pack gyoza wrappers
oil, for frying (groundnut oil
  is good)

FOR THE FILLING

2 skinless, boneless chicken thighs
45g kale, tough stems removed
3 spring onions, trimmed and
  finely chopped
1 clove garlic, crushed
5cm piece of fresh ginger, peeled
  and finely grated or chopped
1 tablespoon chopped
  pickled ginger
1 tablespoon toasted sesame oil
1 tablespoon soy sauce
1 tablespoon rice wine vinegar
1 lime, zest and juice

FOR THE DIPPING SAUCE

3 tablespoons rice wine vinegar
3 tablespoons soy sauce
1 tablespoon toasted sesame oil
juice of ½ lime
1 red chilli, deseeded and very
  finely chopped
2 spring onions, very finely
  chopped
2cm piece of fresh ginger, peeled
  and finely chopped

1. Put the chicken thighs into a food processor and blitz until they form a rough paste.

2. Place a steamer in a pan and steam the kale until soft. Drain and squeeze dry. Once cooled, finely chop and add to a large bowl with the rest of the filling ingredients. Mix until everything is well combined.

3. Place a wrapper on a clean surface and have a small bowl of water nearby. Place a heaped teaspoon of the mixture in the middle of the wrapper and moisten the edge with water (using your finger). Fold the wrapper in half over the filling and pinch it in the centre. Starting at the centre (where you have pinched the wrapper together), carefully pleat the wrapper to the end, then pleat to the other side. Continue until you have used up all the filling or made as many as you think you will need. Keep on a plate covered with cling film in the fridge if you are not cooking these straight away.

4. Make the dipping sauce by mixing all the ingredients together in a bowl.

5. To cook, heat a little oil in a frying pan over a medium heat. When hot, add the gyozas in batches and lightly pan-fry the bottoms for a minute or two before flipping over to crisp the tops. (Alternatively you can steam the gyozas for 6 minutes.)

6. Devour the gyozas with the dipping sauce.

Saffron Roasted Peppers
and Tomatoes, Crispy Chickpeas and Buckwheat with Labneh

Labneh – or strained yoghurt – is a beloved accompaniment in the Middle East and luckily it's easy enough to make at home. This really is one of our favourite dishes to feed a crowd. It plays on complementary textures and flavours: smooth with crunch, sweet with tart, and spice with soothing labneh.

Serves 6–8 as a side

4 red peppers, halved and deseeded

large handful of small mixed tomatoes (approx. 20)

few sprigs of thyme

1 tablespoon harissa

large pinch of saffron threads

2 cloves garlic, sliced into thin chips

4 tablespoons olive oil, plus a glug for frying

1 tablespoon balsamic vinegar

1 tablespoon soft brown sugar

½ x 400g tin chickpeas, drained and rinsed (120g drained weight)

2 tablespoons buckwheat

small bunch of coriander, finely chopped

sea salt and pepper

FOR THE LABNEH
1kg natural yoghurt
1 teaspoon sea salt

FOR THE SPICY NUTS
4 tablespoons olive oil
1 teaspoon fennel seeds
1 teaspoon nigella seeds
2 teaspoons coriander seeds, crushed
1 teaspoon cumin seeds
2 teaspoons roughly chopped pine nuts
2 teaspoons chopped hazelnuts
1 teaspoon chilli flakes

1. First make the labneh. Line a deep bowl with a double layer of cheesecloth (or a clean dishcloth). Stir the yoghurt and salt together and place in the centre of the cloth. Pull the corners of the cloth up to make a ball and tie closed tightly with string. Suspend over a bowl to collect the liquid (a cupboard handle works well) or set in a sieve over a bowl. If the weather is hot do this in the fridge. Let this hang while you get on with the rest of the recipe (or overnight if you have time).

2. Preheat the oven to 180°C/gas 4 and line a baking tray with baking paper. Place the peppers and tomatoes on the lined tray and scatter with the thyme sprigs. In a small bowl, mix together the harissa, saffron, garlic, olive oil and balsamic vinegar and season well. Drizzle this over the peppers and tomatoes, mixing in with your hands. Finally sprinkle the sugar over the top and roast in the oven for 45 minutes.

3. Heat a good glug of olive oil in a large frying pan over a medium heat. When hot add the drained chickpeas and buckwheat with a good sprinkle of sea salt and fry for about 5 minutes, stirring occasionally, until golden and crisp. Remove with a slotted spoon and drain on kitchen paper.

4. Now for the spicy nuts. Heat the olive oil in a small frying pan over a medium heat and add all the spices, chopped nuts and chilli flakes. Sizzle for 3–5 minutes until the spices have crisped. Remove from the heat and set aside.

5. When the peppers and tomatoes are out of the oven and cool enough to handle, peel the skins off the peppers and place the flesh in a mortar and pestle with the juices collected in the tray. Pound together to form a coarse, loose paste.

6. Serve by dolloping the labneh onto a large plate. Spoon the peppers over, then dot the tomatoes about sporadically, followed by the crisped chickpeas and buckwheat, then the spicy nuts (with all the delicious oil). Finish with a scattering of chopped coriander.

FOR THE FISH

350g skinless cod fillets

2 limes, zest and juice

2 cloves garlic, crushed

½ teaspoon ground cumin

½ teaspoon ground coriander

2 tablespoons olive oil, plus extra
for frying

small bunch of coriander, stalks
chopped, leaves left whole

FOR THE GREEN SAUCE

4 tomatillos

5 jalapeño slices (from a jar)

1 clove garlic

5 spring onions, white parts only

small bunch of coriander

½ teaspoon ground coriander

½ teaspoon ground cumin

FOR THE MAYONNAISE

3 chipotle chillies in adobo

6 cloves black garlic

2 handfuls of walnuts

4 tablespoons mayonnaise

juice of 1 lime

1 tablespoon olive oil

FOR THE SLAW

½ pink grapefruit, skin and pith
removed with a sharp knife and
flesh cut into segments

½ bulb fennel, thinly sliced

½ red onion, thinly sliced

2 radishes, thinly sliced

small bunch of coriander,
chopped

few sprigs of mint, leaves
chopped

drizzle of olive oil

TO SERVE

lime wedges

soft tacos

1 avocado, stone removed,
peeled and sliced

sour cream

coriander and mint leaves

sliced chillies

Fish Tacos
with Tomatillo Salsa and Smoky Walnut and Black Garlic Mayonnaise

We love, love, *love* fish tacos (we love all tacos, but especially fish ones). In fact we love Mexican food – it is all about the sauces, the smoky chillies, the fun sides and the feast of taste and colour – they do it so right. There is a really good online shop called coolchile.com, where we get totally carried away. It's so fun, they have every sort of chilli, every sort of potion, they even have a tortilla press (yes we bought one) and *tortilleros* – pretty baskets with lids for keeping tortillas in (yes we bought some, and no we have never used them).

This is a fresh and easy marinated fish taco with a bright green zingy sauce and crunchy slaw. Tomatillos, chipotle chillies in adobo and black garlic are available from most large supermarkets, or online.

1. Place the cod in a non-metallic dish. Mix all the remaining ingredients for the fish together and pour over the cod, then set aside.

2. Prepare all the accompaniments: put all the green sauce ingredients into a food processor or blender and whizz together until almost smooth, then transfer to a pretty bowl; whizz all the smoky mayo ingredients in a food processor and transfer to another bowl; mix the slaw ingredients together in a bowl.

3. Heat a pan over a medium–high heat and add a little olive oil. Add the fish, cook for about 4 minutes to allow the fish to crisp, then flip it over and cook the other side. Add the rest of the marinade and toss the fish, allowing it to break up. Take the pan off the heat and squeeze over a little lime juice.

4. Serve the fish on tacos with the slaw, green sauce and smoky mayo. Add sliced avocado, sour cream, coriander and mint leaves, sliced chillies and a squeeze of lime to serve.

Roasted Cauliflower, Feta and Coriander Frittata
with Spiced Stewed Tomatoes

This is the kind of dinner we love to tuck into on a Sunday night. It's enough to excite and comfort the taste buds, banishing the dreary Sunday blues, but light enough to end what might have been a heavy weekend of consuming.

Memories of frittatas are a bit *comme ci comme ça* – dry, bland and with that awful bounciness of overcooked egg. The key is to not cook them for too long – they should only go into a hot oven for a few minutes, because you want a gooey, soft and delicious inside.

Serves 4

6 eggs, beaten and seasoned

½ cauliflower, cut into small florets

2–3 tablespoons olive oil or coconut oil

1 teaspoon cumin seeds, plus a little extra for the top

1 teaspoon ground coriander

1 teaspoon turmeric

2 limes, zested

2 onions, sliced into thin half-moons

1 clove garlic, crushed

1 green chilli (leave the seeds in if you like it hot), finely chopped

small bunch of coriander, stalks finely chopped and leaves picked and roughly chopped

100g frozen peas

120g feta, crumbled

1 teaspoon nigella seeds (optional)

salt and pepper

FOR THE TOMATOES

olive oil

2 cloves garlic, sliced

½ teaspoon chilli flakes

250g cherry tomatoes

¼ red onion, finely chopped

juice of ½ lime

small handful of coriander, leaves chopped

1. Preheat the oven to 220°C/gas 7 and line a baking tray with foil or baking paper.

2. First make the tomatoes. Heat a little olive oil in a pan over a medium heat and add the sliced garlic and chilli flakes. Cook for a minute, then add the whole tomatoes and cook for a further 10 minutes, stirring occasionally. Once the tomatoes have softened and started to fall apart, remove from the heat and add the onion, lime and coriander.

3. Tip the cauliflower florets onto the baking tray and shake them around with 1–2 tablespoons olive oil or coconut oil, the cumin seeds, ground coriander, turmeric and plenty of salt and pepper. Put into the oven for 8–10 minutes, or until crisp and golden.

4. Melt the remaining oil in a pan over a medium heat and sauté the onion slices until translucent, then add the garlic, chilli and a big pinch of chopped coriander stalks. Cook for a few minutes until beginning to caramelise and then add the frozen peas, stirring to cook through.

5. Next add the roasted cauliflower, half the coriander leaves, half the crumbled feta and the lime zest and pour the eggs into the pan. Stir this all around, making sure everything is combined, then scatter the remaining feta on top evenly with a few extra cumin seeds.

6. Leave on the heat for a few minutes so the base starts to crisp, then transfer the pan to the oven and cook for a few minutes, making sure you keep the inside nice and soft.

7. To remove from the pan, slip a spatula around the edge and then transfer the frittata to a serving plate. Dollop the stewed tomatoes on top of the frittata and add the remaining coriander leaves to the top.

Middle Eastern Spiced Aubergine Gratins

This feels like a decadent and indulgent little number, but actually it's pretty light and healthy. We like to do this in small individual bubbling pots, but of course this can be made in one big dish. This is a perfect hot veggie number to have alone or to accompany other dishes.

Serves 6

8–10 aubergines (depending on size)
1 lemon, zest and juice
200g baby spinach
400g feta, crumbled
100g pine nuts
salt and pepper

FOR THE TOMATO SAUCE
glug of olive oil
bunch of spring onions, finely diced
5 cloves garlic, crushed
1–2 teaspoons chilli flakes
3 x 400g tins chopped tomatoes
1 tablespoon ground cumin
1 tablespoon smoked paprika
1 tablespoon caster sugar
bunch of thyme, leaves picked

FOR THE CREAMY SAUCE
50g butter
3 cloves garlic, crushed
bunch of sage, chopped
500ml crème fraîche
1 lemon, zested
bunch of fresh herbs (chives, coriander and parsley), chopped

1. Preheat the oven to 220°C/gas 7.

2. Pierce the aubergines all over with a knife and place on a baking tray. Roast for 30 minutes, then set aside to cool, but don't turn the oven off. Alternatively, you could scorch them over an open flame from a gas stove, which will give them a nice smoky flavour. Do this until blackened all over. Set aside to cool.

3. Meanwhile, make the tomato sauce. Heat the olive oil in a pan and add the spring onions, garlic and chilli flakes and sauté for 5 minutes. Add the chopped tomatoes, cumin, paprika, sugar and thyme and simmer for about 15 minutes. Season to taste with salt and pepper.

4. Make the creamy sauce. Heat the butter in a small pan and add the garlic and sage. Lightly fry for a couple of minutes and take off the heat – do not let it burn. Add the crème fraîche, lemon zest and herbs and stir to combine.

5. Scoop all of the aubergine flesh out onto the baking tray and tear up with a fork, add the lemon zest and juice and season with salt and pepper. Bake for 10 minutes, until crisp; reduce the oven temperature to 180°C/gas 4.

6. Line up your small ovenproof dishes and start layering. First is a small handful of fresh spinach leaves followed by some tomato sauce, then the pulled aubergine, some creamy sauce and some crumbled feta. Repeat these layers one more time. Finish each gratin with a sprinkling of pine nuts.

7. Bake in the oven for about 20 minutes until hot and bubbling. Serve with flatbreads (see page 265) for dipping.

Sticky Miso Spare Ribs

Ribs are just a lot of fun: messy, succulent, crispy, get-your-hands-dirty-while-outside-in-the-sun kind of fun. It is all about getting good-quality, meaty ribs and a damn good sticky sauce. These ribs are the perfect balance of sticky, sweet and spicy, which makes them extremely addictive. You could call them BBQ ribs, but as there is only about one weekend a year that we can actually get the barbecue out, they can happily be cooked under a grill or in a hot oven for the rest of the year. You want them to be caramelised by the end of the cooking process – for extra finger-licking good times!

Make sure to buy high-welfare pork ribs – not only is it kinder, they taste better too.

1. To make sure your ribs are tender, simmer them first in boiling water for 30 minutes, then drain.
2. Mix all the remaining ingredients together in a large bowl to make a marinade and then add your ribs. Marinate for at least 3–4 hours, or even better, overnight.
3. Once marinated, the ribs can be grilled, barbecued or roasted in a hot oven for 15–20 minutes. We love them best on the barbecue, served with fresh chilli and coriander and accompanied by a crunchy salad.

Serves 4–6

2 racks of pork ribs
3 tablespoons miso paste
3 tablespoons maple syrup
1 tablespoon sesame oil
2 tablespoons soy sauce
2 red chillies, deseeded and chopped finely
3 cloves garlic, crushed
5cm piece of fresh ginger, peeled and grated
2 limes, zest and juice
3 tablespoons rice wine vinegar
100ml cloudy apple juice

TO SERVE
sliced red chilli
coriander leaves

Flatbread Pizzas

These are quick and easy pizzas that anyone can make at home – they require no skill or patience and you will be taking them out the oven within 20 minutes, if that. These are our favourite toppings but you could try anything – we think it is pretty impossible to go wrong with pizza toppings.

These pizzas have really thin and crispy bases and seem to get demolished super-fast, so plan to make more than you think you need! We often serve these as part of a feast, or it's nice to sling them out of the oven when your guests are arriving, to serve instead of canapés.

For the flatbreads, use the recipe on page 265 up to the end of stage 2. Preheat the oven to 220°C/gas 7 and place a non-stick baking sheet or pan in the oven to heat up while you make your toppings. Then take your baking sheet out of the oven and drizzle with a tiny bit of olive oil. Carefully place your rolled-out flatbread on top and after a minute or so bubbles will start forming; flip it and add your toppings to the flatbread before returning to the oven to bake.

All the recipes below make one large flatbread. To turn any of these into a calzone, simply fold your flatbread pizza in half with the toppings inside. Bake in the oven for an extra 2 minutes.

splash of olive oil
½ teaspoon cumin seeds
½ teaspoon coriander seeds, crushed
½ clove garlic, thinly sliced
½ green chilli, finely chopped
100g minced lamb
½ teaspoon ground turmeric
¼ teaspoon ground cinnamon
1 big plum tomato, chopped
pinch of chopped coriander leaves
¼ red onion, sliced into thin rings
1 heaped tablespoon crumbled feta
2 teaspoons pine nuts
½ tablespoon natural yoghurt
1 tablespoon tahini
1 lemon, zest and a little of the juice
salt and pepper

TO SERVE

watercress
pinch of roughly chopped coriander and mint leaves
1 tablespoon pomegranate seeds

Spiced Lamb with Yoghurt, Coriander and Pine Nuts

1. Heat the olive oil in a frying pan and add the cumin seeds and crushed coriander seeds. When fragrant, add the garlic and chilli and stir for a minute, then add the minced lamb. Keep breaking it up, allowing the meat to crisp a little. Then add the turmeric, cinnamon and tomato and cook until the tomato breaks up into a sauce. Remove from the heat, add the chopped coriander and season well.

2. Spread the lamb mixture over the flatbread, followed by the sliced red onion, crumbled feta and pine nuts. Cook in the oven for 8–10 minutes. Meanwhile, mix the yoghurt and tahini with the lemon zest and a little squeeze of lemon juice.

3. Serve by scattering the watercress, coriander, mint and pomegranate seeds over the top and drizzle with the tahini dressing.

White Pizza with Tenderstem Broccoli, Garlic and 'Nduja

½ tablespoon olive oil, plus extra for drizzling

1 tablespoon ricotta

½ lemon, zested

5 basil leaves, chopped, plus extra for garnish

1 small clove garlic, crushed

2 teaspoons 'nduja

5 Tenderstem broccoli spears, lightly steamed (but still crunchy)

¼ large buffalo mozzarella ball

salt and pepper

1. In a bowl mix together the olive oil, ricotta, lemon zest, chopped basil and garlic. Season with salt and pepper.

2. Spread the ricotta mixture evenly over the flatbread so that it nearly reaches the sides, then dot little blobs of 'nduja all over. Place the broccoli sporadically around, then tear up the mozzarella and scatter on top.

3. Cook for 5–8 minutes until bubbling and golden. Tear up a little more fresh basil for the top, add a good drizzle of olive oil and serve immediately.

Harissa, Goat's Cheese, Red Onion and Coriander

2 teaspoons harissa mixed with 2 teaspoons chopped tinned tomatoes (or just use 1–2 tablespoons of our Smoky Harissa – see page 259)

¼ red onion, thinly sliced

50g goat's cheese, crumbled

small bunch of coriander, leaves picked

1. Spread the harissa over the flatbread, then sprinkle with the red onion and goat's cheese.

2. Cook for 5–8 minutes until the cheese is starting to turn golden. Remove from the oven and scatter with the coriander leaves.

Wild Mushroom and Taleggio

splash of olive oil, plus extra to drizzle

1 clove garlic, sliced

4 large portobello mushrooms, cleaned and sliced

big pinch of roughly chopped rosemary leaves, plus extra for the top

small squeeze of lemon juice

big pinch of parsley leaves, plus extra to garnish

1 heaped tablespoon roughly chopped taleggio

½ large red chilli, deseeded and roughly chopped (or use chilli oil)

small handful of rocket

sea salt and pepper

1. Heat the olive oil over a medium heat and start frying the sliced garlic. As it starts to turn golden, add the sliced mushrooms and rosemary. Keep stirring and cooking down for a few minutes – you want the mushrooms to turn golden. Squeeze in the lemon juice and add the chopped parsley. Remove from the heat.

2. Spoon the mushrooms over the top of the flatbread, followed by the taleggio pieces, sliced chilli and the extra pinch of rosemary. Cook in the hot oven for 5–8 minutes.

3. Serve immediately scattered with the rocket and extra parsley on the top and a sprinkle of olive oil, sea salt and pepper.

This pizza is also delicious with a tomato base.

More Flatbread Pizza Ideas

Brunch:
spinach, mozzarella,
spring onions,
Parmesan, ham
hock, poached egg,
chopped chilli

———

Autumn:
thinly sliced butternut
squash, blue cheese,
red onion, thyme,
honey, rocket

———

Artichoke hearts,
spicy fennel salami,
mozzarella,
black olives

———

Capers, anchovies,
mozzarella,
chopped chilli, parsley

———

Spicy sausage,
smoked mozzarella,
roast garlic, tomato,
oregano, basil

Hair-of-the-dog:
roasted red peppers
and cherry tomatoes,
harissa, chorizo, smoked
Cheddar, basil,
chopped chilli

———

Ratatouille:
red onion, roasted
red pepper, aubergine,
black olives, garlic,
rosemary, torn
buffalo mozzarella

———

Red grape,
rosemary, pecorino,
chilli flakes

———

Spinach, nutmeg,
roasted garlic,
mozzarella,
feta, oregano

———

Courgette, ricotta,
basil, chopped chilli,
cherry tomatoes, garlic

Springtime:
goat's curd, courgette,
peas, mint, basil,
pea shoots

———

Griddled aubergine,
tomato sauce,
ricotta, chives,
tarragon, mozzarella

———

Smoked pancetta,
mozzarella, tomatoes,
chopped chilli, basil

———

Chanterelles, butter,
thyme, mozzarella,
chilli flakes, rocket,
lemon, Parmesan

———

Parma ham,
Gorgonzola,
figs, basil

Roast Tomato and Harissa Tart
with an Oat Crust

This recipe has become a real Tart favourite over the years – a 'Tart's tart' one might say! We have cooked it so many times for photo shoots and it never lets us down. It is a much-requested recipe, so here it is! Lucy grew up with this recipe, as it is a favourite of her Mum's (mostly down to the fact that you do not have to blind bake the pastry base. As well as it being totally delicious). It was originally a Jane Grigson recipe, a cook her mother often turned to for inspiration. The recipe comes from her *Vegetable Book*, first published in 1978 and beautifully written, if you are interested.

Serves 8–12

FOR THE BASE

125g plain flour

125g porridge oats

pinch of salt

125g fat (we use a half and half mixture of butter and Trex, but you can use all butter)

1 large egg, beaten

FOR THE FILLING

60g butter

1 medium-large onion, chopped

1 large clove garlic, chopped

1 x 400g tin chopped tomatoes

1 large egg

75–100ml double cream, as needed

1 heaped tablespoon grated Parmesan

60g grated Cheddar, plus extra for the top (optional)

1 teaspoon harissa, or to taste (or use chilli sauce, 1 small seeded chilli or cayenne pepper)

handful of breadcrumbs (optional)

handful of cherry tomatoes, halved

salt

1. Preheat the oven to 190°C/gas 5 and put a baking sheet on the middle shelf of the oven.

2. Put all the base ingredients into a food processor and pulse until just starting to form a dough. Tip out and press into a 22cm loose-bottomed tart tin, making sure you press into the flutes of the tin – no need to roll out. Put the tart case into the fridge to chill while you make the filling.

3. Melt the butter in a pan over a medium–low heat and cook the onion and garlic until soft but not coloured, about 5 minutes. Tip in the tomatoes and boil hard until fairly thick and not at all watery. Break the egg into a measuring jug and add enough cream to bring up to 150ml; mix well.

4. Remove the tomato mixture from the heat and stir in the cheeses and then the egg and cream mixture. Add the harissa gradually to taste – add more if you think it needs to be hotter. Season with a little salt.

5. Turn the tomato mix into the pastry case and top with a little grated Cheddar and the breadcrumbs. Arrange the halved cherry tomatoes, cut side up, on top and then place the tart case on the preheated baking sheet and bake for 30–40 minutes, or until nicely golden on top and slightly bouncy when touched. Allow to cool before serving.

Salads and
Vegetables

By far the best part of shopping at food markets anywhere is marvelling at and poring over the displays of vegetables: different shades of tomatoes stacked high, deeply hued courgettes and beetroot, white-tipped radishes, beautiful mottled-pink borlotti beans, piles of crisp runner beans, spiky-layered fat artichokes and fur-lined broad bean pods. Vegetables are a magical, intriguing gift from the natural world. Their beauty and qualities so deserve celebrating, and we do. Deciding what to make with the vegetables we've bought is, for us, pure culinary excitement: raw and crunchy, roasted and caramelised, griddled and crisp, barbecued and smoky, creamy and cheesy; any which way can be a sensation.

Vegetables grown nearby, so you get them freshly harvested and in their right season, are the best – packed full of flavour, and better for you too. It is so important to support your local greengrocer (ours is Parkway Greens in Camden Town, London), who most likely uses suppliers that are closer to home than those who provide for the supermarkets. British produce is hugely varied and abundant and we live in a time when more and more people are celebrating locally grown, seasonal food. There's no need to eat asparagus flown in from the Netherlands or beans from Brazil.

Vegetables are a magical, intriguing gift from the natural world.

And of course, if you can, growing your own vegetables is a deeply rewarding experience – even if it's just some herbs or rocket in a window box. Watching them grow, cutting, preparing, cooking and eating them gives you an extraordinary sense of wholeness, and helps you develop a new respect for the processes that provide us with what we eat. The production and distribution of food has become a very complicated thing in our modern world, with industrial farming, pesticides and chemicals, mechanised processing and preservation and long distance transportation. All of these things erode the basis of food culture everywhere, as well as the natural world and our health. Growing your own, in whatever way you can, is a way of inspiring positive change in the world.

We always encourage people to buy ugly vegetables, too. Huge amounts of food go to waste every day, and in the case of vegetables (and fruit) a large part of that due is to an unwillingness to buy produce that isn't visually 'perfect'. Misshapen carrots, beetroot and swedes are thrown away and wasted. We support the initiatives that are sprouting up to bring ugly vegetables to the market, from Rubies in the Rubble to Morrisons' line of 'wonky' vegetables. So don't be afraid of a less-than-perfect specimen – it's the little steps that make all the difference.

Crispy Artichoke Salad

Brown Rice Salad

Buffalo Mozzarella and Roasted Black Grape Salad

Roast Tomato and Quinoa Salad

Shaved Brussel Sprouts

Tart Salad

Raw Courgettes and Buffalo Mozzarella

Smoked Tomatoes, Burrata and Basil Oil

Seared Fillet of Beef Carpaccio

Crispy Chicken Salad

Chicken Noodle Salad

Hot-smoked Salmon Salad

Summer Charred Mackerel Salad

Baked Ricotta with Mixed Tomatoes

Crispy Kale

Griddled Fennel

Blistered Courgette

Caramelised Butternut Squash Carpaccio

Hot and Sticky Aubergine

Crispy Winter Vegetables

Grilled Aubergine and Roast Feta

Roast Baby Beetroot

Roast Sweet Potatoes

Crispy Artichoke Salad
with Capers and Parmesan

Artichokes – they look almost prehistoric. They are also pretty versatile. We often serve them raw, carpaccio-style with lemon juice and very good olive oil. Or there is the delectable way of eating them by tearing off the juicy leaves and dunking them into a buttery sauce. Occasionally we marinate them and char them on the barbecue.

However wonderful though, sometimes the thought of prepping them can feel a bit daunting. You can get decent artichoke hearts that have been ready-prepared in jars, and although good ones are not cheap, some kind person has done all the hard work for you. This is a tasty and naughty little cheat using ready-prepared hearts.

1. Heat the olive oil in a frying pan, but don't let it get too hot.
2. Add the artichokes to the pan with the garlic and rosemary and fry on each side until crisp and golden.
3. Mix together the lemon zest and juice, balsamic vinegar, extra virgin olive oil, chopped capers and sliced shallots to make a dressing.
4. Arrange the rocket on a round serving plate and add the crispy artichokes, garlic and rosemary. Shave over a generous amount of Parmesan, sprinkle with toasted pine nuts, basil and parsley and drizzle over the dressing. Season well with salt and pepper.

Serves 2

1 tablespoon olive oil

200g artichoke hearts, drained and patted dry with kitchen paper

2 cloves garlic, halved

2 sprigs rosemary, leaves chopped

1 lemon, zest and juice

½ tablespoon balsamic vinegar

2 tablespoons extra virgin olive oil

1 tablespoon capers, chopped

1 shallot, very thinly sliced

large handful of rocket

Parmesan shavings

1 tablespoon toasted pine nuts

few sprigs of basil, leaves torn

small bunch parsley, leaves roughly chopped

sea salt and pepper

Brown Rice Salad
with Quick Pickled Beetroot, Maple-glazed Pecans, Peas, Avocado and Mint

This is a great salad; it works as a hearty lunch dish on its own or as part of a spread (it goes very well with chicken). It's a beautiful rainbow of striking pinks and bright greens that really livens up a table and the sour pickle, sweet nuts and smooth avocado create a lovely balance of flavours. You can make the different components ahead of time but to keep the salad fresh and vibrant don't mix everything together until the last moment.

Serves 4

250g brown rice

200g frozen peas

3 tablespoons extra virgin olive oil

bunch of mint, leaves picked and chopped

bunch of chives, snipped

2 avocados, stones removed, peeled and roughly chopped

200g feta, crumbled

bunch of pea shoots

salt and pepper

FOR THE QUICK PICKLED BEETROOT

1 red onion, thinly sliced

2 beetroot, peeled and cut into 1cm cubes

80ml cider vinegar

40g caster sugar

3 bay leaves

1 tablespoon coriander seeds, crushed

1 teaspoon chilli flakes

bunch of fresh oregano, leaves chopped

1–2 tablespoons jarred jalapeños, chopped (optional)

FOR THE MAPLE PECANS

1 tablespoon olive oil

1 tablespoon maple syrup

½ teaspoon cayenne pepper

150g pecans

1. First make the quick pickled beetroot. Put the red onion and beetroot into a bowl. In a separate pan, combine the vinegar, sugar, bay leaves, coriander seeds and chilli flakes. Place the pan over a high heat, bring to a simmer, then turn down and leave to simmer for a few minutes. Remove the pan from the heat, add the remaining ingredients and then pour over the beetroot and onion. Leave to marinate while you prepare the rest of the salad.

2. Now for the pecans. Preheat the oven to 200°C/gas 6 and line a baking sheet with baking paper. Mix together the olive oil, maple syrup and cayenne pepper, add the pecans and stir to coat. Tip onto the lined baking sheet and put into the oven for 10–15 minutes until bubbling and toasted. Take out and leave to cool.

3. Bring a small pan of water to the boil and add the brown rice with a good pinch of salt. Cook according to the packet instructions, then drain and cool.

4. Plunge the peas into boiling water for 30 seconds, then drain.

5. Mix together the rice, the beetroot mixture (remove and discard the bay leaves), peas, extra virgin olive oil and herbs and season with salt and pepper. Break up the maple pecans and scatter over the salad with the avocados and gently fold through. Finish with the feta and pea shoots and serve immediately.

Buffalo Mozzarella and Roasted Black Grape Salad
with Crispy Prosciutto and Smoked Sea Salt

We can't remember why we first thought of roasting grapes, but we are so glad we did – they are quite delectable. We use them on a bruschetta that we have been making for years that combines roasted grapes with goat's cheese and a drizzle of truffle oil – they are pretty and different. Here we are pairing them with creamy buffalo mozzarella, basil and crispy Parma ham – when you get a mouthful of this with all the elements together, it's one of those moments when you just stop for a second and think 'God, that's delicious'.

Serves 2

small bunch of seedless black grapes

small bunch of thyme

drizzle of olive oil, plus extra for frying

1 slice of Parma ham, roughly torn

small handful of salad leaves

1 buffalo mozzarella ball

50g roasted hazelnuts

1 red chilli, sliced

pinch of smoked sea salt (optional)

drizzle of peppery extra virgin olive oil

drizzle of good-quality balsamic vinegar

few basil leaves

few edible flowers (optional)

salt and pepper

1. Preheat the oven to 220°C/gas 7 and line a baking tray with baking paper or foil.

2. Pull the grapes off the stems and place on the baking tray with the thyme. Drizzle with olive oil, season with salt and pepper and roast for about 20 minutes until the grapes are sizzling. Remove from the oven and leave to cool.

3. Heat a little more oil in a small frying pan and fry the pieces of Parma ham until crisp, then remove and drain on kitchen paper.

4. Scatter the green leaves over a serving plate, tear up the mozzarella and dot over the top (you could also leave the mozzarella whole). Scatter over the grapes, hazelnuts, chilli and Parma ham pieces. Season with the smoked salt, if using. Drizzle over a little peppery extra virgin olive oil and balsamic and finish with a few basil leaves and some edible flowers, if using. Serve at once.

Serves 5–6

6 sweet plum tomatoes (large and small), halved

2 teaspoons smoked paprika

2 tablespoons olive oil, plus extra for drizzling

squeeze of honey

3 cloves garlic, crushed

pinch of fresh thyme leaves (optional)

1 bulb fennel, roughly sliced lengthways

6 spring onions, sliced lengthways

200g chorizo, cut into 2cm rounds

200g quinoa

small bunch of rocket or spinach

2 avocados, stones removed, peeled and sliced

10 asparagus spears, woody ends snapped off, steamed for 4–5 minutes and sliced

3 eggs, soft-boiled for 5 minutes, then peeled and halved

100g soft goat's cheese, crumbled

small bunch of coriander leaves

2 tablespoons toasted flaked almonds

2 tablespoons shelled pistachios

2 red chillies, deseeded and finely chopped

sea salt and pepper

lemon wedges, to serve

FOR THE YOGHURT DRESSING

4 tablespoons natural or Greek yoghurt

2 teaspoons each of ground coriander and cumin

1 clove garlic, crushed

good pinch of finely chopped mint leaves

1 lemon, zest and juice

FOR THE LEMON AND HONEY DRESSING

4 tablespoons olive oil

juice of ½ lemon

squeeze of honey

1 tablespoon apple cider vinegar

Roast Tomato and Quinoa Salad
with Asparagus, Chorizo, Avocado and Toasted Almonds

This is the kind of dish we would love for either lunch or dinner; it's the perfect all-round balanced salad – deliciously filling and an ideal mix of textures, colours and flavours. We often serve it when catering for photo shoots, beautifully presented on big serving platters – it looks so exciting to dig into, though works very well on individual plates as well.

If it all seems a bit much for a speedy lunch, you could make it quicker by including just your favourite components, but if you have the time it is well worth the effort.

1. Preheat the oven to 220°C/gas 7 and line a baking tray with baking paper (to save on washing-up).

2. Arrange the tomato halves on the tray. Mix together the smoked paprika, olive oil, honey, garlic and thyme, if using, and drizzle this all over the tops of the tomatoes. Place the tray in the oven to roast for 30 minutes.

3. Put the sliced fennel, spring onions and chorizo on a separate baking tray, spreading them out to give them room. Drizzle with olive oil and season. Place in the oven for at least 20 minutes, turning half way through the cooking. You want it to be caramelised and charred.

4. Rinse the quinoa thoroughly and then cook according to the instructions on the packet (we like to add a little powered stock and lemon juice to the boiling water for flavour). Once cooked, set aside.

5. Mix all the yoghurt dressing ingredients together in a bowl, and then in a separate bowl mix together the ingredients for the lemon and honey dressing, seasoning both dressings to taste.

6. On a platter or individual plates, toss the rocket or spinach with the quinoa. Layer on the fennel, spring onions, tomatoes, chorizo, avocado and asparagus, and drizzle over the lemon dressing. Top with the soft-boiled egg halves and then add the crumbled goat's cheese, coriander leaves, nuts and chillies. Dollop the yoghurt mix into the middle and serve with a lemon wedge and maybe some griddled sourdough.

Shaved Brussels Sprouts
with Pine Nuts and Goat's Cheese

This is a quick and easy number that is a perfect crunchy side to complement most dishes. It's delicious all year round, too. Brussels are the perfect vegetable for taking on flavour, especially when shredded like this.

1. Preheat the oven to 200°C/gas 6.

2. Put the walnuts and pine nuts on a baking tray and toast for about 5 minutes, or until golden. Allow to cool slightly and then chop them, either by pulsing in a food processor, or on a chopping board with a good old knife.

3. Put your mandoline on a medium setting and shave the Brussels from their tops, widthways. Don't worry about getting to the very ends – save those fingers! If you don't have a mandoline, use a very sharp knife to shred the Brussels.

4. Put the Brussels in a bowl with the goat's cheese, chopped walnuts, pine nuts and dill. Whisk the dressing ingredients together and pour over the salad; season generously to taste (you may need to add a little more olive oil).

Serves 4–6

handful of walnuts

2 tablespoons pine nuts

15 (approx.) Brussels sprouts

60g hard goat's cheese, shaved

1 heaped tablespoon chopped dill

FOR THE DRESSING

1 tablespoon Dijon mustard

1 tablespoon honey

1 tablespoon white balsamic vinegar (or normal balsamic if you can't get hold of white)

juice of ½ lemon

3 tablespoons extra virgin olive oil, plus extra if needed

1 shallot, finely chopped

sea salt and pepper

Tart Salad

There's quite a lot riding on this, seeing as it is named the Tart Salad. We didn't deliberately call it that; it just got the name and stuck. It's a salad we have been making since day one. We can even remember how it came about. We were sitting in Lucy's kitchen scribbling down menus for the following week, starving and in need of some lunch, joking about how we cook for a living yet there were only four things in the fridge – half a jar of homemade tomato chutney, an avocado, some lamb's lettuce and goat's cheese. After finding pine nuts in the cupboard, lunch was quickly assembled. It worked, and it found itself on the next week's menu… and the week after that… and four years later it is still on most of the lunch menus we do.

1. Arrange the lamb's lettuce on a platter or individual plates. Mix the olive oil, lemon juice and salt and pepper together, then drizzle over the lamb's lettuce; toss to coat.

2. Carefully arrange the avocado slices over the lettuce, then dot over the tomato chutney – you want pretty little dots, not sparse chunks.

3. Next is the goat's cheese; using your hands break off little bits of the goat's cheese and scatter over the salad.

4. Finally, scatter over the pine nuts and finish with a drizzle of olive oil.

Serves 4–6 as a side

1 bag of lamb's lettuce

3 tablespoons extra virgin olive oil, plus extra for drizzling

juice of ½ lemon

2 large avocados, stones removed, peeled and thinly sliced

½ jar of tomato, ginger and chilli chutney (we recommend using ours on page 259, but understand if you have to buy it just this once)

1 small log (approx. 200g) soft goat's cheese without the rind (keep in the fridge until needed)

25g toasted pine nuts

salt and pepper

Raw Courgettes and Buffalo Mozzarella
with Broad Beans and Mint

This is such a pretty summer salad; quick to put together and very pleasing on the eye. It's a nice one to have as a sharing starter – you'll want to dig in with a piece of toasted sourdough. If you close your eyes while taking a mouthful, you'll be transported to a summer garden; think about the summer light shining through the sweet peas, the fresh smell of basil in the air and the sounds of happy, busy bees.

1. First deal with the broad beans. Bring a small pan of water to the boil and add the beans; simmer for a few minutes, then drain and refresh under cold water. Squeeze the beans out of their skins.

2. In another pan of boiling water, blanch the peas for a couple of minutes then drain and refresh under cold water. Set aside.

3. Use a potato peeler to peel the courgette into long ribbons and then divide between two plates. Squeeze a little lime juice over and toss to coat.

4. Scatter over the broad beans, radishes, pea shoots, mint, basil and chilli in a pretty fashion. Squeeze over the remaining lime juice.

5. Gently tear the mozzarella and divide between the two plates, drizzle with olive oil and a little honey and season with salt and pepper. Add a few edible flowers, if liked.

Serves 2

200g podded broad beans
200g podded fresh peas
1 courgette
juice of 1 lime
4 radishes, thinly sliced
handful of pea shoots or leaves
small bunch of mint, leaves picked
small bunch of basil, leaves torn
1 red chilli, sliced
1 buffalo mozzarella ball
drizzle of good-quality extra virgin olive oil
drizzle of honey
salt and pepper
edible flowers, to garnish (optional)

Smoked Tomatoes, Burrata and Basil Oil

This is a really fantastic dish. The surprise is the smoked tomatoes, which work famously with the creamy burrata and the freshness of the basil. Do not be put off by the smoking – it really is so much easier than you might think and well worth it, taking the dish to that next level. Make a batch of smoked tomatoes and keep them in the fridge to use in other dishes; they add a wonderful depth when added to salads or dressings. See page 271 for more on smoking.

1. Cut the tomatoes in half and drizzle with olive oil, red wine vinegar and season with salt and pepper.

2. If you are smoking your tomatoes, set up the smoker using maple woodchips, following the instructions on page 271.

3. Once wisps of smoke start to appear, open the smoker and place the tomatoes inside. Close the lid and smoke for 15–20 minutes over a low heat. Take off the heat and leave to cool.

4. To oven roast the tomatoes, put the prepared tomatoes into a baking dish and roast at 200°C/gas 6 for 20–30 minutes.

5. Make the basil oil. Place the basil, garlic and extra virgin olive oil in a food processor and blitz. Squeeze in the lemon juice and season with salt and pepper.

6. Arrange the rocket on a dish (if using) and place the tomatoes sporadically on top, then sprinkle over the oregano. Place the burrata in the middle and drizzle over the basil oil. Serve with fresh crusty bread.

Serves 2–3

2 tablespoons maple woodchips
6 plum tomatoes
drizzle of olive oil
drizzle of red wine vinegar
handful of rocket (optional)
small bunch of fresh oregano
  (optional)
1 large burrata ball
salt and pepper
crusty bread, to serve

FOR THE BASIL OIL
large bunch of basil
1 small clove garlic
60ml good-quality extra virgin
  olive oil
juice of ½ lemon

Seared Fillet of Beef Carpaccio

with Crunchy Greens, Crispy Shallot and Garlic and a Vietnamese Dressing

Serves 8

450g beef fillet (we like using fillet tails)

groundnut oil

2 shallots, finely sliced

3 garlic cloves, finely sliced

1 big red chilli, deseeded and finely sliced

mixed baby salad leaves

handful of beansprouts

a couple of radishes, finely sliced

handful of coriander (with stalks)

5 spring onions, sliced lengthways into strips

few torn mint leaves

50g toasted peanuts, roughly chopped

1 tablespoon sesame seeds, toasted

sea salt and pepper

FOR THE DRESSING

4 large lime leaves

5cm piece of fresh ginger, peeled and grated

1 garlic clove, grated

1 shallot, finely chopped

2 red bird's eye chillies, deseeded and finely chopped

big pinch of mint leaves, finely chopped

big pinch of coriander leaves, finely chopped

3 tablespoons fish sauce

2 tablespoons rice vinegar

3 tablespoons lemon juice

2 tablespoons toasted sesame oil

1 tablespoon palm sugar or maple syrup

1 tablespoon soy sauce

We use fillet tails in this recipe (which is just the tail end of the fillet, not the actual tail of the cow). It's a brilliant cut to know about, as it is the same quality as the fillet but a fraction of the price. You wouldn't get very far serving them as the main event as they are pretty small, but they are ideal for a salad. As it is fillet, it is also very lean – exactly what you want in a salad – and is lovely seared in a hot pan; because they are so small there is no need to then cook them in the oven. As well as serving the fillet seared, as we have here, we also sometimes keep it raw.

This works well as a starter or as a sharing platter for a main – it really is delicious. We'd be very happy to be served this at a dinner party, and would most definitely ask for the recipe!

1. Get a griddle pan very hot, to smoking point. Trim the fillet of any fatty bits, then drizzle with oil, season with salt and pepper and rub all over. Sear the beef on all sides to your liking – we like to sear it very quickly (about a minute each side) so it is still very rare in the middle.

2. Slice the beef as thinly as possible across the grain and lay out on a serving plate or individual plates, making sure to leave a circle free in the middle. Cover and put aside in a cool place.

3. Add a good splash of groundnut oil to the same pan over a medium–high heat and, when hot, add the sliced shallots. When they start to colour add the sliced garlic and chilli. Fry for a further few minutes until the garlic chips are golden and crisp. With a slotted spoon, remove the crisped shallots, garlic and chilli onto kitchen paper.

4. Make the dressing. First, remove the stems and central veins from the lime leaves, then roll up and shred them very finely. Add them to a mixing bowl along with the other ingredients and whisk together with a fork.

5. To serve, arrange a handful of leaves and beansprouts in the middle of the plate, followed by the radishes, coriander, spring onions and mint. Drizzle over the dressing, then add the peanuts, sesame seeds, crispy shallots, garlic and chilli. Serve immediately.

Crispy Chicken Salad
with a Smoky Yoghurt Dressing

This is a punchy, full-flavoured and robust salad that will hold its own as a main meal, either for lunch or supper. We often make it heartier by adding roast sweet potato wedges, the sweetness bringing a wonderful balance with the smoky dressing and the fresh herbs.

Don't be put off by how many ingredients there are, it really is quite simple to put together and an exciting salad to serve – the ultimate chicken salad.

Serves 4–6

2 teaspoons dried oregano

juice of ½ orange

1 teaspoon smoked paprika

good squeeze of honey

1 clove garlic, crushed

1 tablespoon ground cumin

½ tablespoon ground cinnamon

6 boneless chicken thighs

splash of olive oil

50g quinoa, cooked according to the packet instructions and drained

large handful of salad leaves

1 avocado, stone removed, peeled and sliced

3 spring onions, thinly sliced lengthways

80g feta, crumbled

small handful coriander leaves

small handful mint leaves

salt and pepper

FOR THE DRESSING

2 tablespoons chipotle in ancho sauce

3 tablespoons Greek yoghurt

1 lime, juice and zest

1 clove garlic

2 teaspoons ground coriander

1. Preheat the oven to 220°C/gas 7 and line a baking tray with baking paper.

2. Mix together the oregano, orange juice, smoked paprika, honey, garlic and ground spices and season with salt and pepper. Pour over the chicken, cover, and leave to marinate in the fridge for at least 1 hour (the longer the better).

3. Blitz all the dressing ingredients together in a food processor or blender, season to taste and set aside.

4. Heat the olive oil in a frying pan and fry the cooked quinoa to create a nice crunchy effect. After a few minutes you will see it crisp up; season well with salt and pepper, remove from the heat and set aside.

5. Remove the chicken from the marinade, reserving the marinade, and put into the lined baking tray. Roast for 25–30 minutes, pouring over the reserved marinade after 20 minutes. Once cooked, slice the chicken into strips, reserving any cooking liquid.

6. Place the salad leaves on a serving platter followed by the avocado, spring onions, strips of chicken, crispy quinoa and crumbled feta. Dollop the dressing over, roughly tear over the coriander and mint and serve.

This is also very nice with grilled corn shaved off the cob, or roasted sweet potato if you want something heartier.

Chicken Noodle Salad
with Peanut, Ginger and Tahini Dressing

This crunchy noodle salad has that downtown summer feel to it and is the perfect lunch on a hot day. It's one of those brilliant dishes that can be prepared ahead of time – all you need to do is mix everything together at the last minute – making it ideal for a picnic, a summer party, or just for taking to work for lunch.

Serves 4

2 chicken breasts

300g vermicelli noodles

drizzle of toasted sesame oil

½ cucumber

1 carrot, peeled and cut into 8–10cm matchsticks

handful of sugar snap peas, sliced lengthways into 3

handful of edamame

2 tablespoons peanuts, toasted and chopped

1 tablespoon toasted sesame seeds

small bunch of coriander leaves with some stalks

small bunch of mint leaves, shredded

FOR THE POACHING LIQUID

1 star anise

2 teaspoons Chinese five spice

2 cloves garlic

5cm piece of fresh ginger, roughly chopped

small bunch of coriander stalks

1 onion, roughly chopped

FOR THE DRESSING

2 tablespoons peanut butter (look for a healthy one or make your own)

1 tablespoon tahini

5cm piece of fresh ginger, peeled and roughly chopped

1 clove garlic

2 red chillies, deseeded

2 tablespoons soy sauce

1 tablespoon toasted sesame oil

1 tablespoon rice wine vinegar

1 tablespoon honey

1 lime, zest and juice

1. First make the poaching liquid: bring a pan of water to a simmer and add all the poaching ingredients. Now add the chicken breasts, reduce the heat, cover and slow-poach for about 20 minutes.

2. Meanwhile, cook the noodles according to the packet instructions, then submerge in cold water, drain, and toss through with a drizzle of sesame oil.

3. Peel the cucumber, leaving tiger stripes. Halve it lengthways and scoop out the seeds, then slice it widthways once, so you end up with 4 pieces. Slice the pieces lengthways as finely as possible into julienne matchsticks.

4. Toss together the noodles, cucumber, carrots, sugar snaps and edamame. Scatter with the peanuts, sesame seeds and herbs, reserving some of each for the garnish.

5. Once the chicken is cooked through (check by cutting into a piece), remove from the poaching liquid and set to one side (save the liquid for the dressing).

6. Put all the dressing ingredients into a food processor or blender and blitz, loosening with about 4 tablespoons of the chicken poaching liquid. Taste to see if you think it needs more spice, or maybe a squeeze more lime.

7. When the chicken has cooled, tear up with your fingers into bite-sized strips and drop into the dressing to soak it up; leave for 5–10 minutes.

8. Mix the dressed chicken with the rest of the salad and scatter with the reserved peanuts, sesame seeds, coriander and mint.

Peas, broad beans or avocado would be nice additions here, too.

Hot-smoked Salmon Salad
with Fennel, Pea Shoots and a Tarragon Dressing

This is perfectly pretty with the light pink of the salmon and the fresh bright green of the crunchy vegetables. The salmon is fantastic and very easy to do – but you must cure it, we have tried cutting corners and it doesn't work. You can get away with curing it for 45 minutes, but it would be even better to leave it for longer. We also love this salmon on a bruschetta with some avocado, lime juice and chilli.

You can use this technique for smoking the salmon for anything else – or any of the recipes in this book that use smoked fish. If you don't have time to smoke your own salmon then you can pick it up at the fishmonger or from the supermarket. It's really worth trying the smoking out yourself if you can, but the salad will still be delicious either way.

Serves 4

400g wild salmon fillet
2 tablespoons soft brown sugar
4 tablespoons sea salt
2 tablespoons alder woodchips
1 bulb fennel
8 asparagus spears
juice of 1 lemon
1 shallot, finely chopped
couple of handfuls of fresh peas, podded
½ bag of pea shoots
extra virgin olive oil

FOR THE DRESSING

3 tablespoons natural yoghurt
juice of ½ lemon
small handful of chopped tarragon leaves
1 teaspoon extra virgin olive oil
salt and pepper

1. Place the fish in a small dish. Mix the sugar and the salt together and press into the fish, making sure both sides are covered. Put into the fridge for at least 45 minutes (the longer you leave it the better; overnight is fine). Take out, rinse and pat dry.

2. Set up the smoker using alder woodchips, following the instructions on page 271. Start to heat the smoker on a low heat, and once wisps of smoke start to appear, open it up and put the salmon fillet inside. Close the lid and cook for 15–25 minutes, depending on thickness. Check after 15 minutes and take it from there – you want it to be still just pink in the centre. Take off the heat and cool.

3. While the fish is smoking, make the dressing; mix all the ingredients together, season well and set aside.

4. Thinly slice the fennel and the asparagus lengthways, then arrange in a dish and squeeze over the lemon juice. Leave for 10 minutes.

5. Assemble the salad by layering the fennel and asparagus, chopped shallot, peas and pea shoots. Add a drizzle of extra virgin olive oil and then flake the hot-smoked salmon on top. Either drizzle the dressing over, or serve it on the side.

Summer Charred Mackerel Salad
with Broad Beans, Asparagus, Watercress and a Caper Dressing

Quite possibly our favourite salad in the book, this hits just the right notes. It is easy to prepare and is a wonderfully happy lunch – it really tastes of spring with the fresh asparagus, broad beans and mint and is both delicate and vibrant. It feels special enough to eat for lunch all the way through spring and summer. Try to find sustainably sourced mackerel.

Serves 2–4

3 large sprigs of rosemary
drizzle of olive oil
1 clove garlic, crushed
2 mackerel fillets
6 (approx.) new potatoes
2 sprigs of mint
10 (approx.) whole broad bean pods, podded
small bunch of thin asparagus spears, woody ends snapped off
6 quail's eggs
2 big handfuls of watercress
1 tablespoon toasted pine nuts
salt and pepper

FOR THE DRESSING
1 tablespoon capers
1 tablespoon chopped tarragon leaves
sprig of mint, leaves picked
squeeze of lemon juice
3 tablespoons extra virgin olive oil
½ tablespoon Dijon mustard
squeeze of honey

FOR THE LEMON CRÈME FRAÎCHE
2 tablespoons crème fraîche
1 lemon, zest and juice

1. Remove the leaves from the rosemary sprigs and finely chop them, then add to a mortar and pestle with a little olive oil and the crushed garlic and pound until you get a paste. Add a little more olive oil and some salt and pepper. Pour this over the mackerel fillets and marinate for at least 30 minutes.

2. Boil the potatoes with the sprigs of mint until cooked, about 10 minutes (test them by prodding with a knife). When they are cooked, drain and return to the pan and bash them around a little with some olive oil, salt and pepper to break them up.

3. Now cook the mackerel. It's delicious cooked on a barbecue, but otherwise cook it under a hot grill, skin side up, for 8 minutes, or until charred and crispy. Set aside.

4. Boil the broad beans for 5 minutes, then drain and slip the individual beans out of their skins. Meanwhile, steam the asparagus over simmering water for 3–4 minutes and then slice lengthways.

5. Cook the quail's eggs in boiling water for 3 minutes, then drain and plunge into cold water to stop them cooking further (so that the yolks stay runny inside). Peel when cool enough to handle.

6. Make the dressing by pounding the capers in a mortar and pestle with the tarragon, mint, a little squeeze of lemon juice, olive oil, mustard and honey. In a separate bowl mix together the crème fraîche, lemon zest and a good squeeze of lemon juice.

7. Toss the watercress with the broad beans, asparagus, potatoes and dressing. Pile onto a big serving plate with the mackerel, breaking it up a little in your hands, then add the eggs, halved lengthways, pine nuts and little dollops of the lemon crème fraîche.

Baked Ricotta with Mixed Tomatoes

Serve 4–6 as a side

1 x 250g tub ricotta

880g seasonal tomatoes (nice to have a mix of sizes, bigger ones cut into chunks)

3 cloves garlic, roughly chopped

5–6 sprigs of thyme, leaves picked and stems discarded

generous glug of extra virgin olive oil

1 lemon, zested

pinch of chilli flakes

sea salt and pepper

griddled sourdough, to serve

This is such a simple recipe, but goodness it is delicious. It's perfect as a sharing side dish, but is also excellent as a starter served with griddled sourdough for everyone to tuck into as one big sizzling dip.

1. Preheat the oven to 220°C/gas 7.

2. Tip the ricotta out upside-down into an ovenproof dish and arrange the tomatoes around it. Dot with the garlic and thyme, add a generous glug of olive oil, season and sprinkle with the lemon zest and chilli flakes. Bake in the oven for 20 minutes.

3. This is delicious served hot from the oven, ready to dig in with griddled sourdough and a delicious glass of cold white wine.

Crispy Kale
with Tahini and Honey

Serve 4–6 as a side

250g bag of kale, tough stems removed

drizzle of olive oil

salt and pepper

FOR THE YOGHURT DRESSING

3 tablespoons tahini

2 tablespoons honey

juice of 1 lemon

4 tablespoons natural yoghurt

1 clove garlic, crushed

2 tablespoons toasted sesame oil

3 tablespoons sesame seeds

The way we most often cook kale is roasted in the oven with a little oil, salt and pepper – it's very moreish. It is a nice way to add a light crunch to a salad or soup. Drenched in the tahini dressing along with the toasted sesame seeds, it also makes a remarkable side dish.

1. Preheat the oven to 200°C/gas 6.

2. Tear up the kale leaves and toss with the olive oil, salt and pepper. Scatter a couple of handfuls over a baking tray and roast for 5 minutes. Check throughout cooking and shake the pan – you want it nice and crispy, but be careful, as it burns really easily. Repeat until all the kale is cooked.

3. Combine all the dressing ingredients except for the sesame seeds; taste and season with salt and pepper. Put the sesame seeds into a small dry pan and toast until golden.

4. Place the kale in a bowl and carefully toss with the dressing and sesame seeds. Serve in a pretty bowl.

Griddled Fennel
with Ricotta, Chilli and Basil

Fennel is our desert island vegetable. We love how it changes from being crisp, fresh and aniseedy to caramelised and sweet when roasted. We came up with this recipe when catering for Jemima's sister's exhibition opening. It was pretty full-on, as the opening night was for 450 people who all needed feeding first, followed by a sit-down dinner for about 100. We paired this fennel dish with lamb, which worked beautifully.

1. Place a griddle pan over a high heat.
2. Chop off the base of the fennel and slice the bulbs into wedges, reserving the feathery parts. Toss the fennel slices in the olive oil and salt and pepper, then lay them on the griddle pan until nicely charred on both sides – you might need to do this in batches.
3. In a small bowl, mix together the ricotta, lemon zest and some salt and pepper.
4. Scatter the rocket leaves on a serving platter, then arrange the griddled fennel on top. Squeeze over the lemon juice, blob over the ricotta mix and scatter with the chilli slices and basil leaves. Finally drizzle with very good peppery extra virgin olive oil.

Serves 6–8 as a side

4 bulbs fennel
1 tablespoon olive oil
250g ricotta
1 lemon, zested, plus juice of ½
100g rocket
1 large red chilli, sliced
small handful of basil leaves
salt and pepper
drizzle of extra virgin olive oil

Blistered Courgette
with Feta, Pomegranate and Dill

Courgette is delicious cooked this way. It's a good one for the barbecue – over white-hot coals it cooks quickly, giving you a slight crunch in the middle with charred outsides. It means that you can get these cooked first and put them back in the marinade to soak up the flavours while the coals cool to embers so you can cook your meat. Neither of us are barbecue experts (we possibly could be if we were allowed near the thing). This could be about to change, as Jemima now has a really fantastic, all-singing all-dancing barbecue, which will cook anything from a steak to a pizza. We have been using it just outside the back door, really as an extra oven, like they do in lovely hot countries where you spend the summer cooking your meals outdoors.

If you are not going to light up your barbecue then you can easily cook this dish under a hot grill.

1. Slice the courgettes lengthways, about 1cm thick, and place them in a flat dish.
2. Whisk up the dressing ingredients and pour over the courgettes, making sure they are all coated. Cover and place in the fridge to marinate for at least 30 minutes.
3. Prepare the barbecue or preheat the grill. Place the courgette slices on/ under the heat for 5 minutes, until blistered – its fine if they turn a little black. Turn the courgettes over and repeat. Remove from the heat and return to their dish, then carefully turn them over so they get a good coating in the marinade once more.
4. Sprinkle with the feta, dill, basil, spring onions, pomegranate seeds and almonds.

Serves 4 as a side

2 courgettes
100g feta, crumbled
small bunch of dill, chopped
small bunch of basil, leaves chopped
3 spring onions, sliced
100g pomegranate seeds
50g toasted flaked almonds

FOR THE DRESSING
120ml extra virgin olive oil
juice of 1 lemon
2 cloves garlic, crushed
small bunch of basil, leaves chopped
salt and pepper

Caramelised Butternut Squash Carpaccio

with Basil and Parsley Salsa, Pumpkin Seeds and Crème Fraîche

Deep, powerful flavours with vibrant and vivacious colours make this dish really stand out. The butternut squash turns almost to caramel as it chars in the hot oven, which, when balanced with the fresh green salsa and the tangy crème fraîche, makes it sing. You will definitely be asked for the recipe.

1. Preheat the oven to 220°C/gas 7 and line a baking tray or trays with baking paper.

2. First make the marinade. In a small pan heat the butter and olive oil, add the honey, cinnamon, nutmeg, cayenne and thyme. The moment it begins to bubble remove from the heat and season well.

3. Give the squash a good clean – you don't need to peel it for this recipe (always a relief) but you do need to chop it up. We find it easiest to cut it about halfway down, at the end of the round bit. Slice both pieces in half and scoop out the seeds from the rounded parts. Then take the pieces and slice them finely on a mandoline; if you don't have one you can achieve this with a sharp knife, by slicing as thinly as possible. Put these pieces into a large bowl, pour the marinade over and massage through with your hands. Season with salt and pepper and leave for at least 10–15 minutes.

4. Make the salsa by blitzing everything together in the food processor; taste and adjust the seasoning.

5. Place the squash on the prepared baking tray (or trays) in a single layer. Roast in the oven for 10–15 minutes. To make it extra crisp on top, it's nice to place it under a hot grill for a few minutes at the end. When the squash is out of the oven, place the pumpkin seeds on a tray and roast in the oven for no more then 5 minutes.

6. To serve, scatter the squash over a serving platter, drizzle over the green salsa prettily, blob with the crème fraîche and finish by sprinkling over the toasted pumpkin seeds and red chilli.

You can make this in advance and serve at room temperature – just assemble when you are ready to eat.

Serves 6

1 butternut squash

FOR THE MARINADE
2 tablespoons butter
1 tablespoon olive oil
generous squeeze of honey
1 teaspoon ground cinnamon
½ teaspoon grated nutmeg
½ teaspoon cayenne pepper
few sprigs of thyme
salt and pepper

FOR THE BASIL AND
PARSLEY SALSA
30g parsley
30g basil
1 clove garlic
5 tablespoons olive oil
2 tablespoons white wine vinegar
juice of 1 lime
5 spring onions

TO SERVE
60g pumpkin seeds
1 tablespoon crème fraiche
  or sour cream
1 large red chilli, deseeded
  and sliced

Hot and Sticky Aubergine
with Goat's Curd, Coriander Oil and Pomegranate Seeds

Irresistible. Sticky, sweet and punchy, this is the kind of dish that makes you go weak at the knees. We could quite happily sit down to a plate of this with just some steamy coconut rice, but we usually serve it as part of a feast. You need all the elements here as the tang of the goat's curd and yoghurt cuts through the sweetness, helped by the lime to balance the dish and the herbs and pomegranate seeds to freshen it.

Serves 4–6

1 large plump aubergine, cut lengthways into 8cm-long wedges

1–2 tablespoons olive oil

2 tablespoons date syrup

1 tablespoon honey

1 clove garlic, thinly sliced

½ tablespoon coriander seeds

100g goat's curd (or soft goat's cheese)

2 tablespoons yoghurt

1 lemon, zest and juice

small bunch of coriander (keep some leaves for garnish)

1 green chilli

1 tablespoon toasted pine nuts

1 tablespoon pomegranate seeds

salt and pepper

1. Preheat the oven to 220°C/gas 7 and line a baking tray with baking paper.

2. Arrange the aubergine on the lined tray and sprinkle with olive oil and salt. Roast for 10–15 minutes, turning once, until golden brown. Toss in a bowl with the date syrup and honey. Reduce the oven temperature to 180°C/gas 4.

3. Return the sticky aubergine wedges to the baking tray and top with the garlic slices. Return to the oven and cook for a further 10 minutes.

4. Dry roast the coriander seeds and crush in a mortar and pestle. Add to a bowl with the goat's curd, yoghurt and lemon zest. Season to taste and set aside.

5. Blitz the bunch of coriander (stalks and all) in a food processor or blender (if you don't have one then use a mortar and pestle), with the lemon juice, green chilli and a good glug of olive oil. Season to taste.

6. Lay the aubergine on a serving dish (holding back the garlic chips for the top). Dollop with the goat's curd, then the green salsa, then sprinkle with pine nuts, pomegranate seeds, the reserved coriander leaves and the garlic chips.

Crispy Winter Vegetables
with Tarragon and Smoked Garlic Sauce

The sauce for this dish is luxurious and rich, and there is something pretty magical about it when it is scooped up with the caramelised cabbage and other bitter greens. We would usually serve this for dinner with a roast chicken, or it is also very good with salmon. We plonk them both in the middle of the table with a green salad and let everyone dig in. It's guaranteed that every last bit of sauce will be mopped up.

Serves 6

250g butter

4 tablespoons white wine vinegar

2 banana shallots, finely chopped

2 cloves smoked garlic, finely chopped

bunch of tarragon, leaves chopped

3 egg yolks

4 tablespoons water

juice of ½ juice lemon

1 teaspoon Dijon mustard

handful of Brussels sprouts, quartered

bunch of kale, tough stem removed and leaves torn

bunch of spring onions, trimmed

1 white cabbage, cut into wedges (keep the core attached so the slices stay together)

drizzle of olive oil

sea salt and pepper

½ teaspoon smoked salt (optional)

1. First clarify the butter. Heat it in a small pan over a medium heat until foaming, then remove from the heat and leave to stand for a couple of minutes. Pass through a fine sieve into a bowl, discarding the solids.

2. Pour the vinegar into a separate small pan and heat gently with the shallots, garlic and tarragon. Lightly cook for a few minutes until soft, then leave to cool.

3. Whisk the egg yolks and water into the vinegar mix and keeping whisking over a very low heat for 8–10 minutes. Then whisk in the clarified butter, lemon juice and Dijon, and season with salt and pepper; set aside.

4. Bring a large pan of water to the boil and lightly blanch all the vegetables for 30 seconds–1 minute. Preheat the grill to high.

5. Arrange the vegetables on a large tray, drizzle with olive oil and sprinkle with salt and pepper, then blast under the grill for a couple of minutes until starting to char.

6. Spread the sauce on the bottom of a serving platter, then arrange the vegetables on top. Sprinkle with the smoked salt, if using, or sea salt and serve straight away with some very good bread.

Grilled Aubergine and Roast Feta
with Tomato Salsa

We serve aubergine like this a lot when catering for large parties because you can prepare everything in advance. Once the sliced aubergines are cooked you can leave them to one side at room temperature for a good few hours while you get the rest of lunch ready – there's no need to refrigerate. It really is a pretty side dish with the slices layered over a serving platter and drizzled with the red sauce and specks of white feta. We also serve it without the tomato sauce and instead drizzle it with a spiced yoghurt and add some pomegranate seeds for colour.

You can substitute the tinned tomatoes for smoked tomatoes (see page 111) for an amazing depth of flavour. Sweet ripe tomatoes in season would also be delicious – nothing beats a perfectly ripe tomato.

Serves 6

3 aubergines, sliced into 1cm rounds
drizzle of olive oil
1 tablespoon za'atar
200g feta
juice of ½ lemon
pinch of dried oregano
small bunch of basil
salt and pepper

FOR THE TOMATO SAUCE
knob of butter
1 onion, chopped
2 cloves garlic, chopped
small bunch of coriander, leaves picked and stalks chopped
2 x 400g tins chopped tomatoes
1 tablespoon harissa

1. Preheat the oven to 220°C/gas 7.
2. Place the aubergine slices on a baking tray and drizzle with olive oil. Sprinkle with the za'atar and season with salt and pepper. Roast for 20–30 minutes until turning a nice golden colour. Remove from the oven and leave to cool.
3. Line a baking tray with baking paper. Place the whole slab of feta on the tray, drizzle with olive oil and squeeze over the lemon juice. Scatter a little oregano over along with some salt and pepper and place in the oven. Roast for about 20 minutes until golden on the top and starting to melt at the sides.
4. Meanwhile, make the tomato sauce. Melt the butter in a pan, add the onion, garlic and coriander stalks and sauté over a medium heat for about 5 minutes until soft and starting to caramelise. Add the chopped tomatoes and harissa, season and simmer for a few minutes.
5. Arrange the aubergine rounds on a serving platter and drizzle over the tomato sauce. Carefully break up the warm feta and crumble over. Sprinkle over the coriander leaves and serve.

If you are preparing it in advance, this dish is fine served at room temperature – the feta will firm up a little, but will still be delicious.

Roasted Baby Beetroot
with Wasabi Yoghurt

This is a very pretty way of serving beetroot. You want to get baby ones with their leaves still on, ideally about the size of a golf ball. If we can, we get a mixture of golden, candy and English beetroot. Sevket at Parkway Greens in Camden, where we get our groceries, is amazing at sourcing the best quality fruit and vegetables. His shop is an Aladdin's cave, full to bursting of the most beautiful vegetables you have ever seen, a juicy rainbow of exotic goods: lilac cauliflowers next to ruby red Romano peppers, emerald green wild garlic in spring and mottled pink borlotti beans in the summer. It is here that we find multicoloured beetroot. It is worth a trip to London just for a visit to his shop.

If you can't find baby beetroot then just buy large ones and slice them into wedges.

Serves 4 as a side

8 baby beetroot (with their
    leaves on, if you can find them)
olive oil
salt and pepper

FOR THE MISO DRESSING
3 tablespoons miso
1 tablespoon honey
3 tablespoons groundnut oil
2 tablespoons rice vinegar
2 cloves garlic, crushed
juice of 1 lime
2.5cm piece of fresh ginger,
    peeled and finely chopped

FOR THE WASABI YOGHURT
4 tablespoons yoghurt
2 tablespoons wasabi paste
1 lime, zested

TO SERVE
2 tablespoons toasted sesame
    seeds
3 spring onions, julienned

1. Preheat the oven to 220°C/gas 7.

2. Thoroughly wash the beetroot and the leaves to get rid of any grit. Lay them in a roasting tray and drizzle with olive oil, salt and pepper. Pour in enough water to come about 1cm up the sides of the tray. Cover with foil and put in the hot oven for 10–15 minutes (or slightly longer if your beetroot are bigger).

3. Mix together the miso dressing ingredients in a small bowl and season. Remove the beetroot from the oven, remove the foil and pour out the water. Drizzle the miso dressing generously over the beetroot and leaves. Return to the oven and cook for a further 15 minutes.

4. Mix together the yoghurt ingredients in a small bowl.

5. Take the beetroot out of the oven and sprinkle with the sesame seeds and spring onions. Dollop over the yoghurt and serve.

Roast Sweet Potatoes
with Marsala Wine, Orange and Sumac Yoghurt

Sweet potatoes are fantastically useful and they last for ages – months after the supermarket sell-by date. They are the kind of ingredient you never remember buying, but they are always there lurking in the back of the larder, ready to bring sweetness and colour to any spread. We love that you don't have to peel them – well, we never do anyway, and you can use the excuse that 'the goodness is all in the skins'.

Roasting is one of the more obvious way of cooking sweet potatoes, but they're also brilliant in stews and curries and baking, too – have a go at the muffins on page 52, swapping the pumpkin for sweet potato.

Serves 8–10 as a side

5 small sweet potatoes, halved
   lengthways
100ml Marsala wine
juice of 1 orange
drizzle of olive oil
pinch of za'atar
pinch of sumac
1 orange, cut into wedges
salt and pepper

FOR THE YOGHURT DRESSING
200g natural yoghurt
1 clove garlic, crushed
2 teaspoons sumac
1 lime, zest and juice
squeeze of honey

TO GARNISH
mint leaves
micro coriander
sliced red chilli
pumpkin seeds
quartered figs
sliced spring onions
chopped pistachios
flaked almonds

1. Preheat the oven to 220°C/gas 7.

2. Put the sliced sweet potatoes into a roasting tray. Combine the Marsala and orange juice in a measuring jug and pour over the sweet potatoes. Drizzle with olive oil and sprinkle over the za'atar and sumac. Dot the orange wedges around the roasting tray, season well and roast in the oven for 45–55 minutes, until nicely golden (it's okay if it all blackens slightly).

3. Meanwhile, mix all the yoghurt ingredients together.

4. Remove the sweet potatoes from the oven and leave to cool a little before arranging on a serving platter. Drizzle over the yoghurt dressing and top with whichever garnishes you fancy.

You can roast the sweet potatoes and orange wedges in advance – just make sure you drizzle over the yoghurt and garnish just before serving

---

Soups and
One-pots

This chapter sums up
how we cook…we like to
make one big, flavoursome
pot and then provide lots
of sides and toppings so
people can create their
own dish.

This chapter sums up how we cook. Fun, sharing, interactive dishes with lots of thought given to colour and texture. It's all about easy preparation and getting ahead when entertaining or cooking for numbers. This is how we cook when we are catering for fashion shoots, how we cook when we have friends round, and how we cook when we are home in the evening and just want to make something super-simple and straightforward. Whether it's for five people or 50 we approach it in the same way.

We like to make one big, flavoursome pot and then provide lots of sides and toppings so people can create their own dish. We call them 'interactive stations' on photo shoots. Whether it is a pho noodle soup, pasta or curry, each one will come with options and toppings to make it fun and customisable to your own taste. Let's say we are having a gang round on a Saturday and decide to serve a dal, something that we could have made in advance and that is full of flavour. Then on the side, depending on the number of guests, we would serve crunchy salsas, chutneys, steamed rice, homemade dosas, yoghurt, herbs and roasted and spiced vegetables. The bigger the amount of guests, the more numerous the sides.

One-pot dishes are the perfect way to build a menu – start with one dish and then think about different colours, textures, and flavours, building it up so that you have a beautiful spread of vibrant small dishes, as varied or as simple as you like. There's more about our menu-planning process on page 19.

Restorative Shiitake Mushroom Broth

Spicy Chilled Avocado Soup

Green Goddess

Pea, Courgette and Basil Soup

Drunken Mussels

Crab and Fennel Bisque

Lemon Sole and Tofu Broth

Almond and Okra Indian Soup

Prawn and Pork Wonton Soup

Tahini Broth with Spicy Ground Pork

Aubergine Dal

Cardamom and Turmeric Chicken Curry

Smoked Haddock Curry

Pheasant, Porcini and Cavolo Nero Risotto Soup

Harissa, Sweet Potato and Tomato Stew

Savoury Oatmeal

Ravioli

Tart's Mac 'n' Cheese

Ragùs

Restorative Shiitake Mushroom Broth

We make this soup all the time – it has been in our recipe bank for years and is still up there with our favorites. It's a soup that is often requested, not just because it is absolutely delicious, but because it is packed with goodness. Full of ingredients to soothe and restore, it is a year-round winner.

Inspired by our travels to Asia, there is a bit of everywhere in this warming bowl – tastes that take us straight back to the bustling streets of Vietnam or the white beaches of Thailand. There is a long ingredients list here, but this isn't a recipe that needs to be strictly adhered to – add or subtract as you please. We both make it in different variations, Jemima with coconut milk and Lucy without.

When serving to a large group of people, we make it more of a thing by adding lots of fun toppings – you want garnishes that will give a good crunch like radishes, edamame or bok choy.

Serves 4

2 shallots
5cm piece of fresh ginger, peeled
2 red chillies
3 cloves garlic
2 lemon grass sticks
stalks from a bunch of coriander
1 tablespoon coconut oil
1 teaspoon ground coriander
1 teaspoon ground cumin
1 teaspoon ground cinnamon
3 lime leaves
500g mixed mushrooms (we use shiitake, quartered, and enoki)
2 limes, zest and juice
800ml stock (vegetable or chicken)
1 teaspoon tamarind paste
handful of dried porcini mushrooms
1½ teaspoons palm sugar (or maple syrup)
1 teaspoon fish sauce
1 tablespoon soy sauce, plus extra for the tofu
300g firm tofu
splash of groundnut oil
splash of toasted sesame oil

TO SERVE
200g dried rice noodles
sliced spring onions
sliced radishes
sliced chilli
edamame
coriander leaves
toasted sesame seeds

1. Blitz the shallots, ginger, chillies, garlic, lemon grass and coriander stalks in a food processor to make a paste, or finely chop by hand.

2. Heat the coconut oil in a pan and add the paste. Sauté for 5 minutes, then add the ground spices, lime leaves, mixed fresh mushrooms and lime zest and cook for another 2 minutes, stirring to make sure it doesn't burn.

3. Next add the stock, tamarind paste, porcini mushrooms, palm sugar, fish sauce, soy sauce and lime juice. Simmer on a medium heat for at least 20 minutes to allow the soup to infuse with all the flavours.

4. Meanwhile, pat the tofu dry on kitchen paper and cut it into cubes. Heat the groundnut oil in a pan and shallow-fry the tofu for a few minutes until crisp and golden before adding a splash of soy sauce and sesame oil.

5. Cook the noodles according to the packet instructions. Divide between warmed deep bowls and pour over the broth, mushrooms and tofu. Add as many of the topping suggestions as you like, finishing with a few coriander leaves and some toasted sesame seeds.

Spicy Chilled Avocado Soup
with Fresh Crab

We first tried chilled avocado soup in New York on a hot summer's day, sitting outside with a glass of cold white wine watching the world go by, a memory which we have been happy to savour. Cold soups conjure up feelings of balmy Mediterranean lunches followed by a siesta, and we would like this soup to create such happiness for you, too. It is a full-flavoured summer soup – velvety smooth and fun with a punchy bright green colour: a wonderful weekend lunch. Avocado soups are quite rich, so smaller portions are usually enough. It's fun to take to the park in a flask, although we might leave the crab behind on that occasion. If you are serving it without crab, add a little crunch with diced cucumber, red onion, mint and coriander.

Serves 4–6

500g chicken or vegetable stock

4 spring onions, washed and trimmed

1 clove garlic, peeled

5cm piece of fresh ginger, peeled

2 green chillies, or to taste

1 x 400ml tin coconut milk

1 cucumber, peeled

1 avocado, stone removed and peeled

4 large green tomatoes

2 teaspoons ground cumin

2 teaspoons ground coriander

small bunch of coriander

small bunch of mint

squeeze of honey

2 limes, zest and juice, or to taste

salt and pepper

FOR THE CRAB

250g crabmeat (you can use both brown and white meat, but we prefer white here)

3 spring onions, finely chopped

1 lime, zested

small bunch of coriander, leaves shredded

small bunch of mint, leaves shredded

GARNISH IDEAS

coriander leaves (micro herbs are great)

sliced radish

sliced spring onion

1. To make the soup, simply place all the ingredients into a blender and blitz until smooth. It is important to taste and season to your liking, as it could need a little more lime for zing, more salt, or maybe even more chilli (we always add more). Pour into a bowl and chill in the fridge for at least a few hours.

2. Meanwhile, mix all the crab ingredients together in a bowl; taste and adjust the seasoning.

3. Once the soup is chilled, serve with a dollop of the crab mixture and sprinkle over your chosen garnishes.

Green Goddess

This noodle soup is a good mid-week number, when you have neither the time nor the inclination to spend hours in the kitchen. It's the dish we turn to when we can't think what to cook, because it is a brilliant way of getting your greens in. It also takes about 15 minutes to put together.

We came up with the recipe as a healthy brunch dish, which is why we suggest serving it with a poached egg (extra points for the added protein) but it soon turned into a go-to dinner dish, too (you can swap the egg for steamed fish or chicken). It's a favourite with our girlfriends, who love the fact that it's a healthy green dish that tastes so good. We made it recently with hot-smoked salmon (see page 116); it worked famously.

Serves 2–3

SOUPS & ONE-POTS

drizzle of olive oil or coconut oil

1 leek, chopped into rounds

2 cloves garlic, finely chopped

thumb-sized piece of fresh ginger, peeled and chopped

1 green chilli, deseeded and finely chopped

½ teaspoon ground turmeric

90ml sherry or white wine

500–750ml chicken or vegetable stock

2 teaspoons white miso paste

½ lime, zest and juice

squeeze of honey (optional)

noodle of choice (we like edamame fettuccine)

1 poached egg per person (see page 38)

handful of your choice of herbs (coriander, mint, basil and Thai basil all work nicely)

salt and pepper

chopped red chilli, to garnish (optional)

FOR THE GREEN VEGETABLES (CHOOSE 3–4, A HANDFUL OF EACH)

broccoli florets

baby spinach leaves

cavolo nero, tough stems removed and roughly chopped

kale, tough stems removed and roughly chopped

edamame

peas

broad beans

sugar snap peas, roughly sliced

French beans, roughly sliced

asparagus spears, roughly sliced

1. Heat the olive or coconut oil in a large frying pan over a medium heat. Add the leek, garlic, ginger and chilli and sauté until slightly coloured, being careful not to burn the garlic. Add the turmeric and stir over the heat for a minute or so.

2. Add the sherry, stock, miso paste and lime zest and juice and simmer for a few minutes to reduce. Season to taste with salt and pepper and add honey if you think it needs a little sweetness.

3. Bring a small pan of water to the boil and cook the noodles according to the packet instructions. Meanwhile, poach the eggs (see page 38).

4. Add your chosen greens to the mixture in the pan, stirring so everything is submerged. Cook for about a minute – you want the greens to stay crunchy. Taste and season as needed. Add the chopped herbs, saving a pinch to garnish.

5. Divide the cooked noodles between warmed bowls, ladle over the greens and broth, then carefully lay on your poached egg. Sprinkle with salt and pepper, the reserved herbs and some chopped chilli, if using. Serve immediately.

Pea, Courgette and Basil Soup

This is a vibrant, fresh, summery soup. We feel like it should be eaten on a balmy afternoon under the shade of a tree on a table dressed with white linen, a bottle of chilled white wine and wild flowers picked from the meadows. Sadly this most probably will not be the case; instead we will be eating it in a small flat as the rain pounds the windows – but we can still dream.

This is a soup that you want to make quickly to keep the colour vibrant. Overcooking will dull the tones and make it muddy. It couldn't be prettier served with a swirl of sour cream and a scatter of edible flowers.

Serves 3–4

drizzle of olive oil

bunch of spring onions (reserve 2 for the topping), roughly chopped

2–3 cloves smoked garlic, chopped (or use regular garlic)

1 courgette, cut into chunks

500ml stock

250g peas (frozen are fine)

bunch of basil

bunch of mint, woody stalks removed

juice of ½ lemon

pinch of grated nutmeg

salt and pepper

TOPPING IDEAS

grated Parmesan

sliced spring onions (see above)

1 courgette, cut into small chunks and fried in olive oil until nice and crunchy

basil, mint or chives

chopped red chilli

dollop of crème fraîche

Parma ham strips, fried until crisp

sourdough croutons

1. Heat the olive oil in a pan over a medium heat and add the spring onions and garlic. Sauté for a good few minutes until starting to caramelise, then add the courgette. Cook for 5–10 minutes, or until the courgettes are softening and starting to colour. Stir occasionally to make sure the garlic does not burn.

2. Add the stock to the pan and bring to a simmer, then stir in the peas and leave for 1 minute. Take off the heat, transfer to a blender and whizz until smooth – make sure it's really whizzed so it doesn't feel gritty.

3. Add the basil, mint, lemon juice, nutmeg and a good amount of salt and pepper, then whizz again. Taste and adjust the seasoning; if has cooled too much, then return to the pan to reheat gently.

4. Serve with any of the suggested toppings (we think Parmesan is a must).

Drunken Mussels

You have got to be ruthless when it comes to mussels, unless you want to learn the hard way. After returning from the fishmonger (with sustainable mussels, if you can) you need to tip them out into a bowl of water; any shells that are not tightly squeezed closed have got to go, and any which have taken a bash are out, too. There is something quite therapeutic about sorting mussels; the tap trickling as you pull our their beards.

This is a pretty fun recipe. The main ingredients are along the lines of a Bloody Mary, so it's a winner already, and the mussels work really well with it, in the same way that some people like to add clam juice to their cocktail to make a Bloody Caesar. Mussels are best in the autumn and these are just the flavours you want at that time of year: warming, slightly spicy and comforting. We would serve this with a loaf of fresh crusty bread and nothing else.

Serves 2–3

1kg mussels, de-bearded
splash of olive oil
1 onion, finely chopped
3 cloves garlic, finely chopped
2 sticks celery, finely chopped
3 bay leaves
1 glass (175ml) sherry
1 glass (175ml) vodka
1 teaspoon celery salt
2 x 400g tins chopped tomatoes
1 x 400ml tin beef consommé
2 teaspoons Tabasco, or to taste
1 teaspoon Worcestershire sauce
1 teaspoon sugar
juice of 1 lemon, or to taste
50ml double cream
bunch of parsley, leaves
  roughly chopped
salt and pepper

1. Wash the mussels thoroughly, discarding any that do not close tightly when you tap them with a knife, or which have broken shells.

2. Heat the olive oil in a very large pan, add the onion, garlic, celery and bay leaves and soften over a medium–low heat. After about 5 minutes add the sherry and vodka (be careful as this can cause dramatic flames, but they will soon fade away) and simmer for a couple of minutes.

3. Add the celery salt, tomatoes, beef consommé, Tabasco, Worcestershire sauce and sugar and simmer for a good 5–10 minutes, then add the lemon juice and mussels and put a lid on the pan.

4. Steam the mussels for 5 minutes, or until they are cooked and the shells are open, shaking the pan once or twice during this time. Remove and discard any that are not fully open. Stir in the cream and season with salt and pepper. Taste and adjust the seasoning; it might need a little more lemon juice, salt or spice (Tabasco).

5. Ladle into warmed bowls and serve sprinkled with parsley.

Crab and Fennel Bisque

What a palaver. We are afraid there are no short cuts, but this recipe is definitely worth it. Once you have got yourself in the mood for a Saturday afternoon of cooking and pottering around the kitchen, then this recipe is actually very easy and terribly satisfying. It's a show-off number, so save it for a dinner party, and make sure your guests know how much trouble you went to! Plus, it's delicious – really delicious.

Serves 8 as a starter
or 4 as a main

FOR THE STOCK
10 cooked crab claw shells
  (reserve the meat)
30g butter
2 onions, roughly chopped
3 sticks celery, roughly chopped
2 teaspoons fennel seeds
1 teaspoon chilli flakes
3 bay leaves
100ml brandy

FOR THE SOUP
knob of butter
1 onion, chopped
2 cloves garlic, chopped
2 bulbs fennel, chopped
1 teaspoon fennel seeds
1 large glass (250ml) white wine
2 litres crab stock
bunch of tarragon
juice of 1 lemon
salt and pepper

FOR THE CRAB
crab claw meat (see above)
2 tablespoons mayonnaise
1½ lemons, zested, plus juice
  of 1, or to taste
1 bulb fennel, grated
1 red chilli, chopped

1. First you need to retrieve the crabmeat from the claws. Crack the claws by using a shellfish cracker (or a hammer) Carefully remove the crabmeat and put it into a bowl; reserve the cracked shells. Cover the bowl, put it in the fridge and save for later.

2. Melt the butter in a large pan over a medium heat and add all the ingredients except for the brandy and the claw shells and sauté for 5 minutes. Add the brandy and the shells and combine. Add enough water to cover the shells generously, cover and simmer for about 1½ hours. Strain.

3. Now for the soup: in a pan large enough to fit all of the soup, melt a knob of butter and add the onion, garlic, fennel and fennel seeds and sauté until starting to caramelise. Add the white wine and simmer for a moment, then stir in the stock and combine. Remove from the heat and pour the mixture into the blender (or use a hand-held stick blender) and blend until smooth. Add the tarragon, lemon juice and salt and pepper and blend again. Return to the pan and keep it warm until ready to serve.

4. Remove the crabmeat from the fridge; you will need about 50g per person if serving as a starter and 100g per person if serving as a main. Add the mayonnaise, lemon zest and juice, fennel, chilli and seasoning. Carefully fold together and taste – add more lemon juice or seasoning if needed.

5. When you are ready to serve, reheat the soup and divide between bowls. Add a good spoonful of the crab mixture to the middle of the soup.

Lemon Sole and Tofu Broth

This is a light, clean soup that's healthy and flavoursome and takes its inspiration from Japan. We love Japanese cooking – the simplicity brings a pleasant change to our hectic lives – and the fact that it is deeply ingrained with tradition. Japanese knives are magnificent (all of our favourite knives are Japanese).

1. Cut both the fish and the tofu into chunks and arrange in a dish. Mix the marinade ingredients together and pour over the fish and tofu, cover with cling film and set aside.

2. Heat the coconut oil in a pan over a medium heat. Add the shallots, ginger, garlic and chilli and sauté for 5 minutes. Finely chop the coriander stalks and add to the pan.

3. Add the miso paste to the pan and stir it in, followed by the stock, rice wine and cinnamon. Gently simmer for 10 minutes.

4. Add the lime zest and juice and taste to see if you think it needs the honey. Season.

5. Add the fish and tofu to the soup and cook for another few minutes. Serve in warmed bowls with the coriander leaves and spring onions scattered on top.

Serves 4

600g skinless lemon sole fillet
   (check for any small bones)
100g silken tofu
1 tablespoon coconut oil
2 shallots, sliced
5cm piece of fresh ginger, peeled
   and chopped
2 cloves garlic, chopped
1 green chilli, chopped
bunch of coriander (leaves
   and stalks)
1 teaspoon miso paste
850ml fish or chicken stock
1 tablespoon Shaoxing rice wine
1 cinnamon stick
1 lime, zest and juice
squeeze of honey (optional)
few spring onions, sliced
salt and pepper

FOR THE MARINADE
1 tablespoon toasted sesame oil
2 tablespoons soy sauce
2 tablespoons Shaoxing rice wine
juice of 1 lime
2 cloves garlic, crushed

Almond and Okra Indian Soup

A light and healthy soup, perfect for boosting the old immune system. This would serve as a good starter for a dinner party, or just a mid-week pick-me-up. It could be made more filling with shredded chicken, or maybe some coconut brown rice, or buttery garlic flatbreads for dipping.

Serves 4

1 tablespoon coconut oil

20 curry leaves

1 teaspoon cumin seeds

1 cinnamon stick

3 shallots, finely chopped

5cm piece of fresh ginger, peeled and grated

4 garlic cloves, thinly sliced

1 green chilli, deseeded and finely chopped

2 teaspoons garam masala

bunch of coriander, stalks finely chopped, leaves torn

1 carrot, finely chopped

1 teaspoon ground turmeric

2 large plum tomatoes, chopped

500ml chicken stock

1 tablespoon tamarind paste

handful of blanched almonds (approx. 100g)

squeeze of lime juice

squeeze of honey

roasted chopped almonds, to garnish

FOR THE SPICED YOGHURT

2 tablespoons yoghurt

1 teaspoon ground cumin

1 teaspoon ground coriander

1 lime, zest and juice

FOR THE ROASTED VEGETABLES

small handful of okra, cut into 1cm rings

1 small aubergine, cut into small cubes

1 large clove garlic, thinly sliced

1 tablespoon flaked almonds

1 teaspoon cumin seeds

drizzle of olive oil

sea salt

1. Preheat the oven to 180°C/gas 4.

2. Heat the coconut oil in a large pan over a medium heat, add the curry leaves, cumin seeds and cinnamon stick and toss until fragrant and the curry leaves are beginning to crisp.

3. Next add the shallots, ginger, garlic, chilli, garam masala, chopped coriander stalks and carrot. Reduce the heat and cook until softened and translucent, 5–8 minutes, stirring frequently. Add the turmeric and chopped tomatoes and cook until the tomatoes form a paste, about 5 minutes, then add the stock and tamarind paste.

4. Soak the blanched almonds in water for up to 15 minutes. Drain, reserving the water, and then blitz in a food processor with a generous cup of the soaking water until it forms a milk. Pour this into the soup and let simmer for 20 minutes.

5. Meanwhile, toss all the ingredients for the roasted vegetables together in a roasting tray and roast for 10 minutes until crisp.

6. Taste the soup and adjust the seasoning with a little lime juice and a squeeze of honey.

7. Mix together the spiced yoghurt ingredients. Serve the soup with the roasted veg on top and swirled with the spiced yoghurt.

Prawn and Pork Wonton Soup

This is comfort in a bowl: exciting, delicious little wontons in a nourishing chicken broth with Sichuan spice. Making your own Sichuan oil makes all the difference and it really is quite simple; it's also delicious to make extra to have with other things. You can buy wonton wrappers in any Asian supermarket or online, or even in some of the bigger supermarkets.

Serves 6–8

splash of olive oil
1 carrot, very finely diced
1 stick celery, finely diced
4 cloves garlic, chopped
5cm piece of fresh ginger, peeled and grated
2 teaspoons Chinese five spice
1 litre chicken or vegetable stock
handful of kale, tough stems removed, leaves shredded

FOR THE WONTONS
180g raw prawns, finely chopped
150g minced pork
small bunch of coriander (stalks and leaves), chopped
2.5cm piece of fresh ginger, peeled and very finely grated
2 cloves garlic, crushed
1 tablespoon toasted sesame oil
1 tablespoon soy sauce
1 tablespoon rice wine vinegar
4 spring onions, finely chopped
1 lemon, zested
36 wonton wrappers

TO SERVE
drizzle of Sichuan oil (see page 260 or use shop-bought)
1 tablespoon toasted sesame seeds
3 spring onions, thinly sliced
1 lime, cut into wedges
small bunch of coriander leaves

1. Heat the oil in a large pan and sauté the carrot, celery, garlic, ginger and five spice in a large pan over a medium heat until soft, about 5 minutes. Pour in the stock and simmer for 20–30 minutes. Add the kale for the last 5 minutes of cooking.

2. Meanwhile, put all the wonton filling ingredients, except the wrappers, in a bowl and mix until well combined. Take a wonton wrapper and place a heaped teaspoon of the filling mixture in the middle. Dip your finger into cool water and draw around the edges of the wrapper to moisten. Fold one corner of the wrapper over to the opposite corner to seal the edges and make a triangle. Holding the wonton in both hands, curl the right-hand corner in first, and then curl the left-hand corner in to meet it. Repeat until you have used up all the filling.

3. Steam the wontons in a steamer for no more than 5–7 minutes.

4. When the wontons are cooked, serve them hot, in warmed bowls (4–6 per bowl). Ladle the hot soup over them and top with a generous amount of Sichuan oil, the sesame seeds, sliced spring onions, lime wedges and coriander leaves.

Tahini Broth with Spicy Ground Pork
Noodles, Soft-boiled Eggs and Sichuan Oil

This is exactly what the doctor ordered when feeling worse for wear after a night on the tiles. We would like this on call the moment our bleary eyes open. Lots of delicious Sichuan spice, pork, an egg and filling noodles… yum!

You can of course buy Sichuan chilli oil, but we really recommend making your own. It's so quick to put together (see page 260), and really makes a big difference to the dish.

Serves 2

3 tablespoons tahini
2 tablespoons chilli bean paste
1 tablespoon rice wine vinegar
good squeeze of honey
1 tablespoon soy sauce
650ml chicken stock
4 spring onions, sliced
2 bok choy, sliced
small bunch coriander, chopped
squeeze of lime juice

FOR THE SPICY PORK
1 tablespoon coconut oil
2 shallots, very finely chopped
5cm piece of fresh ginger, peeled and cut into very thin matchsticks
1 Thai red chilli, deseeded and finely chopped
2 cloves garlic, sliced into chips
big handful of chestnut mushrooms, chopped
1 tablespoon Chinese five spice
300g lean minced pork
1 tablespoon soy sauce
squeeze of honey

TO SERVE
2 eggs
200–300g udon noodles
drizzle of Sichuan oil (see page 260, or use shop-bought)
coriander leaves, to garnish

1. In a pan over a medium heat, stir together the tahini, chilli bean paste, vinegar, honey and soy sauce. Add a little stock at a time until it turns into a smooth paste, then pour in the rest of the stock. Simmer for 15 minutes. Add the sliced spring onions, bok choy, chopped coriander and a squeeze of lime.

2. Meanwhile, heat the coconut oil in a wok. Add the shallots, ginger, chilli, garlic, mushrooms and the Chinese five spice. Cook over a high heat for a few minutes, then add the pork, breaking it up in the pan. When it starts to crisp, add the remaining tablespoon of soy sauce and another squeeze of honey.

3. Boil the eggs in a pan of boiling water for 5 minutes, then plunge into cold water, peel and set aside. Cook the noodles according to the packet instructions.

4. When you are ready to serve, divide the noodles between two warmed bowls. Ladle over the stock, spoon on the spicy pork and top each bowl with 1–2 egg halves. Now the best bit – finish with generous drizzles of Sichuan oil. Scatter with coriander leaves and serve.

If your tahini splits in the stock, this is easily remedied by blitzing it with a hand blender before adding the vegetables

Aubergine Dal
with Crispy Cauliflower, Green Chutney, Dosa and a Crunchy Salad

This is a wonderful dish for a crowd, and if you use vegetable stock it's fully vegetarian. Make a quarter of the amount of just the dal for a quick weeknight dinner for two, or go the whole hog with all the sides if entertaining. Well, we say the whole hog, but actually the sides are quick and easy, and they make such a difference as it's really all about the toppings here – something smoky and nutritious (the cauliflower), something fresh and crunchy (the salad), something creamy and refreshing (the yoghurt) and something crispy for dipping (the dosa). In India the dal is often a side dish, but here it is very happily the main event. You can always add a side of rice, although we feel it is hearty enough already as it is packed with lentils, which are a very good source of protein (make sure you soak your lentils, making it easier on the digestion).

Serves 6–8

1 tablespoon coconut oil

2 onions, chopped

5cm piece of fresh ginger, peeled and grated

4 cloves garlic, sliced

2 cinnamon sticks

1 tablespoon cumin seeds

2 teaspoons coriander seeds, crushed

1–3 (depending on how hot you like it) bird's eye chillies, deseeded and chopped

20 curry leaves

large bunch of coriander, stalks chopped and leaves kept whole

1 tablespoon ground turmeric

1 large aubergine, cubed

handful of dried apricots, chopped

1 x 400g tin chopped tomatoes

1 x 400ml tin coconut milk

500ml chicken or vegetable stock

350g lentils (use a mixture of red, orange and yellow)

squeeze of honey (optional)

salt and pepper

FOR THE GREEN CHUTNEY

2 tablespoons desiccated coconut

5 tablespoons yoghurt

small bunch of coriander

small bunch of mint

1 lime, zest and juice

Continued over page

1. First make the chutney. Put the coconut into a small bowl and just cover with boiling water. Leave for about 20 minutes to cool and soften, then drain and add to a blender with the remaining chutney ingredients. Blitz until smooth. (This is best served after a few hours resting in the fridge.)

2. Now for the dal: heat the coconut oil in a large pan and cook the onions, the ginger, the garlic and cinnamon over a low heat until the onions are translucent. Increase the heat then add the cumin and coriander seeds, bird's eye chillies, curry leaves and chopped coriander stalks and fry for a good 5 minutes, stirring to stop anything catching.

3. Next add the turmeric, aubergine and apricots and cook for a further 5 minutes, allowing the aubergine to caramelise a little, followed by the tomatoes, coconut milk, stock and lentils. Leave to simmer for 45 minutes, then taste and season with salt and pepper and a squeeze of honey, if desired.

4. Meanwhile, make the crispy cauliflower. Preheat the oven to 220°C/ gas 7. Put the whole cauliflower into a large bowl and toss with the olive oil, coriander and cumin seeds, garlic, salt and pepper. Place on a baking tray and roast for about 30 minutes until nice and crispy. (Alternatively you can break the cauliflower into florets before roasting – just as delicious!)

Continued over page

Aubergine Dal
with Crispy Cauliflower, Green Chutney, Dosa and a Crunchy Salad
(*continued*)

FOR THE CRISPY
CAULIFLOWER

1 good-sized whole cauliflower

drizzle of olive oil

1–2 teaspoons each coriander
and cumin seeds, crushed

2 cloves garlic, crushed

FOR THE DOSA

100g gram (chickpea) flour

200ml water

1 teaspoon ground turmeric

1 teaspoon cumin seeds

a little coconut oil

FOR THE CRUNCHY SALAD

½ cucumber, peeled and seeds
scooped out, then roughly
chopped

1 red chilli, sliced

2 plum tomatoes, roughly
chopped

1 small red onion, diced

handful of mint and coriander
leaves

juice of 1 lime

good drizzle of olive oil

FOR THE TARKA

1 tablespoon coconut oil

4 cloves garlic, sliced into
thin chips

1 teaspoon cumin seeds

1 teaspoon nigella seeds

1 large red chilli, thinly sliced

small bunch of curry leaves

5. While the cauliflower is in the oven, prepare the dosa by mixing all the ingredients together in a bowl until combined. Heat a wide frying pan with a little oil (we use coconut oil) over a medium heat. When hot, add a small ladle of the mixture and tilt the pan quickly, to spread the mixture around. Once it starts to crisp and has bubbles (after a few minutes), flip it and cook the other side until crispy. Repeat until you have used up all the batter.

6. Mix together the ingredients for the crunchy salad in a bowl, drizzle with the lime juice and oil and season.

7. When you are almost ready to serve, make up a tarka for the top of the dal. Melt the coconut oil in a pan and add the garlic, cumin seeds, nigella seeds, chilli and curry leaves. Cook over a low heat, stirring, until the garlic turns golden. Add this sizzling to the top of the dal.

8. Scatter the dal with coriander leaves and serve with the dosa, crispy cauliflower, chutney and salad.

Cardamom and Turmeric Chicken Curry

Nothing is more annoying than finding a recipe that you want to whip up that evening, then realising that you have to marinate something for hours – who has the time? We get that, so if you're a bit rushed, you can make this recipe without marinating the chicken for four hours and it will still taste delicious. But if you do have the time, the yoghurt does wonders for the chicken by tenderising it – and you will see the difference.

We got the base of this recipe from visiting Sri Lanka. Both of us fell in love with the country and its food – fragrant, fresh and vibrant curries; just thinking about it whisks us back to the lush coconut-fringed coastline and white-hot sands. Bliss. The best curry we had was down on the beach in a little hut which was run by a husband and wife – the husband caught the fish and the wife cooked them – we ate the most sensational calamari curry, which we have adapted here, swapping the calamari for chicken. Give it a go with calamari, too, if you like (or fish for that matter), just make sure you give it a good squeeze of lime before serving.

Serves 4–6

6 skinless, boneless chicken thighs

1 tablespoon coconut oil

1 large onion, chopped

3 cloves garlic, chopped

5cm piece of fresh ginger, peeled and chopped

1 small green chilli, finely chopped

5 curry leaves

1 teaspoon fenugreek seeds

4 cardamom pods, crushed

1 cinnamon stick

1 tablespoon Sri Lankan curry powder (or any curry powder)

1 x 400ml tin coconut milk

1 lime, zest and juice

1 tablespoon white wine vinegar

squeeze of honey (optional)

FOR THE MARINADE

2 teaspoons ground turmeric

3 cloves garlic

1 lemon, zest and juice

bunch of coriander stalks, stalks chopped and leaves reserved for garnish

100ml natural yoghurt

salt and pepper

1. Place all the marinade ingredients into a food processor, seasoning well, and whizz until smooth. Put the chicken into a non-metallic dish and pour the marinade over, making sure all the thighs are covered. Cover and put in the fridge for at least 4 hours, preferably overnight.

2. Remove the chicken from the fridge 20 minutes before cooking.

3. Heat the coconut oil in a pan over a medium heat, add the onion, garlic, ginger, chilli and curry leaves and sauté for about 5 minutes.

4. Add the dried spices and cook for about 1 minute, then add the chicken and turn to coat in the spices. Cook for 2–3 minutes, then add the rest of the marinade and the coconut milk. Simmer for 10–15 minutes before adding the lime zest and juice and vinegar. Taste and season, adding honey if you think it needs a little sweetness. Scatter over the reserved coriander leaves and serve with rice.

Smoked Haddock Curry
with Coconut and Sweet Potato

Smoked fish works superbly with these flavours and this curry is one of our crowd-pleasers; it's a really good one to have up your sleeve as it's guaranteed to go down well – and is a nice little ego boost too, as everyone always asks for the recipe. It's fragrant and satisfying while also being light and healthy, so you won't suffer from a post-dinner slump like you might after some heavy stews and curries.

We use fresh turmeric here, but if you can't find it then make a paste by mixing the ground version with a little water – just make sure you wear gloves as it seriously stains.

Serves 3–4

1 tablespoon coconut oil

1 large onion, chopped

3 cloves garlic, chopped

thumb-sized piece of fresh ginger, peeled and chopped

1 bird's eye chilli, finely chopped

bunch of coriander, stalks chopped and leaves reserved for garnish

1 teaspoon coriander seeds, crushed

thumb-sized piece of fresh turmeric, peeled and juiced or grated (or use 2 teaspoons ground turmeric, see recipe introduction)

4 lime leaves

1 sweet potato, peeled and chopped into 1cm cubes

2 teaspoons fish sauce

1 large glass (250ml) white wine

1 x 400ml tin coconut milk

500g skinless smoked haddock fillet, cut into large chunks

1 lime, zest and juice

handful of spinach

salt and pepper

TO SERVE

yoghurt

sliced chilli

lime wedges

flatbreads or rice

1. Heat the coconut oil in a large pan, then add the onion and garlic and sauté for a few minutes over a medium heat. Next add the ginger, chilli, coriander stalks, coriander seeds, turmeric and lime leaves and continue to sauté for 5 minutes, stirring occasionally.

2. Add the sweet potato, fish sauce, white wine and coconut milk and bring to a simmer. Simmer for 12–15 minutes until the sweet potato is soft.

3. Add the haddock to the pan, stir carefully and cook for 4–5 minutes, then add the lime zest and juice, spinach and season.

4. Divide between warmed bowls and serve with yoghurt, sliced chilli, coriander leaves, lime wedges and flatbreads or rice.

Pheasant, Porcini and Cavolo Nero Risotto Soup

When cooked right, pheasant is a delicious bird – it is easy to overcook it, when it will become as tough as boots. Lucy grew up in Northumberland where she spent her life living off pheasants through the winter months, always trying to come up with something new. It is a very lean meat and has a delicate gamey flavour. Our favourite way to cook it is gently in a liquid, so it is able to soak up the juices. We like to do this in something called a chicken brick, a large terracotta pot that is fantastic for keeping birds succulent. It acts like a traditional clay oven, sealing in the air and moisture. They are pretty cheap, and easy to pick up online (if you don't have one then use a lidded casserole dish).

Serves 4

knob of butter

1 leek, trimmed and chopped into rounds

2 cloves garlic, finely chopped

few sprigs of thyme

2 bay leaves

200g risotto rice

handful of dried porcini (soaked in boiling water to cover for about 15 minutes)

large glass (250ml) white wine

1 litre stock (use the reserved poaching liquid and top up to make 1 litre or see Tip, below)

1 tablespoon jarred porcini mushroom paste (optional)

squeeze of honey

4–5 cavolo nero leaves, tough central stems removed and leaves roughly chopped

bunch of tarragon, leaves chopped

25g grated Parmesan

salt and pepper

FOR THE POACHED PHEASANT

2 pheasants (or use a small chicken)

1 leek, roughly chopped

3 bay leaves

2 cloves garlic, halved

bunch of thyme

glass (175ml) white wine

glass (175ml) water

1. Put the pheasant into the chicken brick or casserole with all the other poaching ingredients. Place in a cold oven, turn the temperature to 180°C/gas 4 and cook for 1 hour. Don't worry if it's slightly underdone, as you are going to cook it again and you don't want it to be overcooked. Leave to cool in the liquid, then pull the meat from the bones and shred (if you're in a rush use washing-up gloves to protect your hands from the heat). Strain the liquid, discarding the solids, and top up with water or chicken stock to make 1 litre; set aside.

2. Heat the butter in a pan over a medium heat and add the leek, garlic, thyme and bay leaves. Sauté for about 5 minutes, then add the rice and stir to coat in the leek mixture. Add the porcini mushrooms and their soaking liquid, the wine and stock and bring to a simmer.

3. Simmer for 10–15 minutes, stirring occasionally, until the rice is cooked. Add the porcini mushroom paste (if using), honey, cavolo nero and shredded pheasant and season with salt and pepper. Just before serving, stir through the tarragon and Parmesan. We also like to add a drizzle of truffle oil sometimes – it's very good.

When making this recipe we often poach more than one pheasant – if we're going to all the effort we might as well, as the pheasant meat can be used in salads and other dishes. It also means you have more bones to make a proper stock – simply add the bones to a large pan with an onion, some black peppercorns, bay leaves, garlic cloves and a stick of celery. Pour in the poaching liquid, top up to cover with cold water, then simmer for an hour.

Harissa, Sweet Potato and Tomato Stew
with Goat's Curd and Crispy Chickpeas

Serves 2–3

1 tablespoon olive oil

1 onion, chopped

3 cloves garlic, chopped

2 teaspoons coriander seeds

bunch of coriander, stalks chopped and leaves reserved for garnish

4 tablespoons harissa (or use our Smoky Harissa – see page 259)

2 sweet potatoes, cut into chunks

3 large tomatoes, cut into chunks (or use a 400g tin chopped tomatoes)

1 preserved lemon, finely chopped

1 tablespoon tomato purée

glass (175ml) white wine

650ml chicken or vegetable stock

1 tablespoon dried oregano

squeeze of honey

2 large handfuls of kale, tough stems removed, leaves roughly chopped (optional)

salt and pepper

FOR THE GOAT'S CURD

50g soft goat's cheese

50g natural yoghurt

1 clove garlic, crushed

2 teaspoons za'atar

1 lemon, zested

FOR THE TOPPING

drizzle of olive oil

1 x 400g tin chickpeas, drained and rinsed

4 spring onions, sliced into rounds

1 avocado, stone removed, peeled and cut into cubes

small bunch of oregano leaves, chopped

handful of pine nuts, toasted

This stew is a good, comforting weekday dish – simple but effective. The tangy goat's curd is just what it needs to balance the sweetness from the sweet potatoes, and the crunchy chickpeas give texture. They're a fun one to add to other dishes too – they're lovely sprinkled on top of a soup.

1. Heat the olive oil in a large pan over a medium heat, add the onion, garlic and coriander seeds and sauté for about 5 minutes. Add the coriander stalks, harissa, sweet potatoes, tomatoes, preserved lemon and tomato purée and stir well to combine. Add the wine, stock, oregano and honey and leave to simmer for about 20 minutes.

2. In the meantime make the goat's curd: mix together all the ingredients, taste and season.

3. Next make the crispy chickpeas: heat a drizzle of olive oil in a pan until hot then add the chickpeas and fry over a medium-high heat until nice and crispy. Remove from the pan and drain on a plate lined with kitchen paper.

4. Taste the stew and season, adding more harissa if necessary. Once the sweet potato is cooked, add the kale, if using, and cook for another minute. Ladle into warmed bowls and top with a good dollop of goat's curd, the crispy chickpeas, spring onions, avocado, reserved coriander leaves, oregano and pine nuts.

This is delicious with a handful of chopped chorizo added to the pan with the onions and garlic in step 1.

Savoury Oatmeal
with Peas, Dill and Goat's Cheese

This may seem like a funny one, but once you get your head round the idea that it's porridge, then you will be fine. It's a bit like an easy risotto, but lighter and it feels more luxurious as the oats just melt away – we are now obsessed. We guarantee you could make the whole thing in less than 10 minutes and there you have it – an energy-filled, comforting and delicious lunch bowl. Stirring the goat's cheese in just before eating makes it super-creamy.

1. Heat the butter or olive oil – whichever you prefer – in a pan over a medium heat. Add the leek, garlic, thyme and bay and gently sauté for about 5 minutes. Add the white wine, then the stock and bring to the boil, then reduce the heat and simmer for a few minutes.

2. Stir in the oats and simmer for 3–4 minutes before adding the peas and Parmesan.

3. Serve in warmed bowls, sprinkled with the dill and goat's cheese.

Serves 3

1 tablespoon butter or oil
1 leek, chopped
2 cloves garlic, crushed
4 sprigs of thyme, leaves picked
2 bay leaves
glass (175ml) white wine
500ml chicken or vegetable stock
80g porridge oats
100g frozen peas
30g grated Parmesan
bunch of dill, chopped
100g crumbled goat's cheese

Ravioli

We love eating pasta, and we love making it, too. It can seem rather daunting, but it's actually so easy and fresh homemade pasta is so delicious that once you start making it you'll be hooked (see page 266 for our fresh pasta recipe). One of the most fun things to do with your homemade pasta is make ravioli. These are two of our best.

Saffron and Ricotta Ravioli

This is a very special ravioli that is guaranteed to impress your friends. It was inspired by something similar that we had at the enchanting Venetian wedding of Jemima's sister, Quentin; it really blew our minds. The burst of saffron oozing out of the middle followed by the creamy ricotta was so delicious. A year later, sitting in our kitchen making homemade ravioli, this little number came to mind.

Serves 4

1 batch of fresh pasta (see page 266)

FOR THE FILLING
250g ricotta
50g grated Parmesan
2 lemons, zested
1 clove garlic, crushed
small bunch of fresh herbs, leaves chopped (chives, basil and tarragon)
salt and pepper

FOR THE SAFFRON BUTTER
large pinch of saffron threads
2 teaspoons hot water
100g salted butter
1 shallot, finely chopped
1 teaspoon chilli flakes

TO SERVE
olive oil
grated Parmesan
rocket leaves

1. Mix all the filling ingredients together in a bowl and season to taste.

2. Put the saffron threads into a small bowl and try to break them up as much as you can with your fingers, then add the hot water and leave to infuse for a few minutes.

3. Blitz the butter with the shallot, chilli flakes and saffron-infused water in a food processor (or you could do by hand, but make sure you chop the shallot really finely first). Turn onto a big piece of cling film and wrap it up, making a long sausage about 4cm in diameter. Put into the fridge to set.

4. Roll out the pasta following the instructions on page 266, and roll it down to the machine's lowest setting. With your long pasta sheet in front of you, cut out rounds using a ravioli cutter or a 6cm biscuit cutter. Place 1 teaspoon of the ricotta mixture into the centre, and top with a slice of the set butter from the fridge (about 1cm thick).

5. Dampen the edges of the pasta around the filling with water, then sandwich another round on top. Use your fingertips to seal the edges, trying to expel all the air as you go. Keep going until you have used up all the filling.

6. Bring a large pan of salted water to the boil. Carefully lower the ravioli into the water, in batches, and cook for 4–5 minutes; they are cooked when they float to the surface of the water. Drain and serve with a little olive oil, Parmesan and torn rocket.

Smoked Ham Ravioli with Herb Broth

We love serving ravioli in a broth – one of our favourites is crab ravioli in a crab bisque. The ham ravioli we have made here is superb on its own, drizzled with some very good olive oil, but it is worth making the broth if you can – the dark green is a pleasant contrast to the pink ravioli, and the flavours marry perfectly. It's all about the crispy Parmesan, too – try not to skip that step. If you want to shave off a little time you could always use a good-quality vegetable or chicken stock instead.

Serves 4

1 batch of fresh pasta (see page 266)

FOR THE GREEN STOCK
1 litre water
1 onion, roughly chopped
1 leek, roughly chopped
2 sticks celery, roughly chopped
4 cloves garlic
2 bay leaves
2 sprigs each of thyme and parsley
6 sprigs of mint
2 large handfuls of spinach

FOR THE FILLING
2–3 slices of smoked ham
2 tablespoons ricotta
2 teaspoons Dijon mustard
few sprigs of thyme, leaves picked
1 clove garlic, crushed
1 egg, beaten
salt and pepper

TO SERVE
8 dessert spoons grated Parmesan
small handful of pea shoots
100g peas (fresh or frozen), lightly cooked

1. First make the Parmesan crisps. Preheat the oven to 180°C/gas 6 and line a baking tray with baking paper. Place dessertspoons of grated Parmesan on the tray, leaving plenty of space around each one. Put in the oven for about 5 minutes until bubbling and golden, then take out and leave to cool.

2. To make the stock, put all the stock ingredients, except the spinach and 4 of the sprigs of mint, into a large pan and bring to a gentle boil. Simmer for up to 40 minutes until the vegetables are completely tender. Strain the stock, discarding the vegetables, and then return to the heat to reduce down to about 600ml. Add the spinach leaves and remaining mint sprigs, let them wilt down, then blitz in a blender. Strain again, pushing all the liquid through a fine-mesh sieve. Add a tablespoon of the green mixture left in the sieve back to the stock.

3. Put the ham, ricotta, mustard, thyme and garlic into a food processor and pulse until smooth (don't worry about the colour!). Add the egg, season and blitz again.

4. Roll out the pasta following the instructions on page 266 to roll it down to the machine's lowest setting. With your long pasta sheet in front of you, cut out rounds or squares using a ravioli cutter or a 6cm biscuit cutter. Spoon a little of the filling mixture into the centre of each, and brush the edges of the paste around the filling with water, using a pastry brush or your finger. Fold the pasta over the filling to create half-moon or parcel shapes (for larger raviolis, take another round and place over the filling). Press down with your fingers, squeezing out any air and making a seal. Repeat with the remaining filling and ravioli.

5. Bring a large pan of salted water to the boil. Carefully lower the ravioli into the water, in batches, and cook for 3–4 minutes; they are cooked when they float to the surface of the water.

6. Divide the ravioli between bowls. Warm the green stock and ladle over the raviolis, then top with pea shoots, peas and Parmesan crisps.

Tart's Mac 'n' Cheese

Mac and cheese really has to be our ultimate guilty pleasure. It's everything indulgent you could ever hope for – gooey cheese, comforting pasta and a crispy topping, all sizzling away. We both agreed years ago that if we did do a cookbook we would definitely feature our ultimate mac and cheese recipe.

This is just what we feel like when we're in need of comfort on a cold rainy day, or when we just have the blues. It's one of those dishes people almost pretend not to love. But it's had a bit of a makeover recently, and its hard for anyone to resist when seeing it on a menu now.

We highly recommend making our Jalapeño, Cashew and Avocado Dip to go with it (see pages 256 and 259), and also a simple green salad.

Serves 4

300g macaroni
40g butter
20g plain flour
400ml whole milk
2 bay leaves
1½ teaspoons Dijon mustard
pinch of grated nutmeg
250g Cheddar (or use smoked
    Cheddar or Gruyère)
splash of olive oil
8 rashers of smoked streaky
    bacon, roughly chopped
5 spring onions, chopped
2 cloves garlic, crushed
1 teaspoon chilli flakes (optional)
small bunch of thyme, leaves
    picked
bunch of chives, snipped
100g mozzarella, ideally buffalo
150g dried breadcrumbs
salt and pepper
fresh coriander leaves, to serve

1. Preheat the oven to 200°C/gas 6.
2. Bring a large pan of salted water to the boil, add the pasta and cook for a couple of minutes less than recommended on the packet, to keep it al dente. Once cooked, drain and refresh in cold water.
3. While the pasta is cooking, prepare the béchamel sauce. Melt the butter in a large pan over a medium heat, add the flour and stir over the heat for 30 seconds or so. Remove from the heat and very slowly add the milk (doing this slowly is important for the sauce to stay smooth). Return to the heat and add the bay leaves. Continue to stir the sauce until it thickens. To check whether it is done, turn the spoon over and drag your finger down the back; if it stays with a finger mark in the middle, it's ready. Stir in the mustard, nutmeg and cheese and season; set aside.
4. Heat the olive oil in a small frying pan and fry the bacon. Once nice and crispy, add the spring onions, garlic, chilli flakes and thyme and sauté over a medium heat. After a few minutes, remove from the heat.
5. Add the pancetta mixture and the drained pasta to the béchamel, then the chives and season. Pour the mixture into an ovenproof dish, tear the mozzarella over the top and sprinkle the breadcrumbs over that.
6. Bake in the hot oven for 10–15 minutes or until bubbly, crisp and golden on the top. Serve straight away with torn coriander leaves over the top. We have it with a crunchy salad, our Jalapeño, Cashew and Avocado Dip and Smoky Harissa (see pages 256 and 259) but it's equally good eaten all on its own.

Ragùs

We go weak at the knees for ragù – it's probably the first thing that we order in an Italian restaurant, followed perhaps by a vongole or a spicy crab spaghetti. And because we are such pasta addicts, we eat and make it a lot. Ragùs take a little while to cook, but you can leave them simmering away while you do other things, and once you have a big pot done it's great for leftovers. These are three of our absolute favourites.

Pork and Fennel Ragù

This is one of our all-time favourite recipes. We both absolutely love it and cook it for many a different occasion – it's a good one if cooking for large numbers, as it's easy to multiply the recipe. Lucy cooked it for her birthday simply served with pasta and a rocket salad – couldn't have been easier. We also serve it as a brunch dish with a poached egg, spicy salsa verde and oak-smoked polenta.

The fennel works beautifully with the pork and the white wine keeps it light. The trick is to really crisp up the sausagemeat by getting the pan super-hot and cooking in batches; this allows the meat to caramelise rather than stew. Make sure you use good-quality sausages – it really makes a difference.

Serves 4

400g good-quality sausages
glug of olive oil
1 red onion, finely chopped
1 bulb fennel, finely chopped
4 cloves garlic, finely chopped
4 sprigs of rosemary, leaves chopped
4 sprigs of sage, leaves chopped
2 bay leaves
1 teaspoon chilli flakes
1 teaspoon fennel seeds
glass (175ml) white wine
1 x 400g tin chopped tomatoes
1 teaspoon sugar
glass (175ml) vegetable or chicken stock, or water, plus extra if needed
small bunch of basil, leaves chopped
handful of grated Parmesan
salt and pepper

1. Cut a slit into each sausage and squeeze the meat out into a bowl, discarding the skins.
2. Heat a good glug of olive oil in a pan over a high heat and add the sausagemeat. Fry for 10 minutes, breaking the meat down and crisping it up, stirring all the time.
3. Add the onion, fennel and garlic and sauté for 5 minutes. Then add the herbs, chilli flakes and fennel seeds and season generously. Cook for a further 5 minutes, making sure it doesn't catch and burn.
4. Next add the wine, tomatoes, sugar and stock or water. Reduce the heat, cover and cook for about 2 hours until the meat is soft and tender. Keep an eye on it while it cooks – if it starts to look too dry or is sticking to the bottom of the pan, add a touch more stock or water.
5. Finally, add the basil and Parmesan and stir into your cooked pasta of choice.

This is very good with crunchy breadcrumbs scattered over the top.

Beef Shin Ragù with Turnip Mash

Nothing is quite as beautiful as a perfect autumn day: the golden sun hanging low in the sky, crisp leaves underfoot and the smell of pine cones in the air. There is something very satisfying about an autumnal walk – being back indoors with the crackle of the fire by 4.30pm should feel wasteful, but instead it feels comforting and jolly. Autumn days bring long, slow cooking – the gentle smells drifting through the house go hand in hand with this time of year. This is a wonderful slow-cooked dish (and a pretty inexpensive one, too). It's earthy thanks to the porcini and thyme, with warmth from the spices and a balancing sweetness from the prunes.

It may seem funny to bring the old turnip to the table, but it just goes so well with beef, and it's nice to use something that is in such abundance later in the year. If you are not in the mood for turnip, then mashed potato or wet polenta would work well, too.

Serves 4–6

splash of olive oil

1kg beef shin, boned and cut into chunks (if possible, ask your butcher for the bones; they will add depth to the dish)

1 onion, roughly chopped

1 leek, roughly chopped

1 bulb fennel, roughly chopped

8cm piece of fresh ginger, peeled and roughly chopped

4 cloves garlic, roughly chopped

2 bay leaves

1 bunch of thyme, leaves picked

1 heaped teaspoon ground cinnamon and 1 cinnamon stick

½ teaspoon cayenne pepper

1 teaspoon cumin seeds

½ bottle (375ml) white wine

850ml beef or vegetable stock

large handful of dried porcini mushrooms, soaked for 10 minutes in boiling water

200g chestnut mushrooms, chopped

200g pitted prunes

FOR THE TURNIP MASH

2 turnips

4 cloves garlic

1 bunch of thyme, leaves picked

drizzle of olive oil

25g butter

50g crème fraîche

salt and pepper

TO SERVE

100g roasted pecans

bunch of coriander, chopped

natural yoghurt

1. Preheat the oven to 220°C/gas 7.

2. Heat a splash of oil in a large, lidded casserole over a high heat and sear the beef pieces so that they are browned all over, then remove from the pan. Reduce the heat and add the onion, leek, fennel, ginger, garlic, bay leaves and thyme. Sauté for 5 minutes until softened.

3. Add the cinnamon, cayenne pepper and cumin seeds and stir to release the flavours, then return the meat to the pan and add the wine, stock, porcini and it's soaking liquid and the beef shin bones, if using. Cover with the lid and simmer gently for 3–4 hours, or until the meat is falling apart.

4. In the meantime make the mash. Put the turnips, garlic and thyme in a roasting tin, drizzle with the olive oil and season with salt and pepper. Roast in the oven for 20 minutes. Transfer to a food processor with the butter and crème fraîche and pulse to combine. Taste and adjust the seasoning.

5. Once the meat is tender, remove the bones and discard, then add the fresh mushrooms and prunes, season and cook for a further 10 minutes.

6. To serve, add a generous dollop of turnip mash to deep warmed bowls. Spoon over the ragù and top with the pecans, coriander and yoghurt.

Lamb Neck Ragù with Chimichurri

We prefer our ragùs to be on the lighter side, rather than rich and heavy – although once in a while an *osso bucco* is heaven. We use lamb neck for this recipe as it is so tender, plus it's inexpensive, which always helps. This dish almost feels quite summery with the basil chimichurri – ragùs aren't just for cold, dark nights in!

Chimichurri is a South American herby salsa that goes really well with grilled meat, but we love it on top of this rich stew. We serve this with a rich and cheesy polenta, but it's equally delicious with pasta if the thought of standing whisking up polenta fills you with dread.

Serves 4–6

splash of olive oil
900g lamb neck, chopped into chunks
1 onion, finely chopped
4 cloves garlic, finely chopped
2 sprigs of rosemary, leaves chopped
2 sprigs of thyme, leaves chopped
bunch of sage, chopped
1 stick celery, chopped
1 bulb fennel, finely chopped
250g chestnut mushrooms, chopped
1 teaspoon chilli flakes
1 x 400g tin good-quality chopped tomatoes
250ml white wine
500ml chicken stock
1 tablespoon redcurrant jelly

FOR THE BASIL CHIMICHURRI
bunch of basil
bunch of parsley
bunch of of mint, leaves picked
1 green chilli
2 cloves garlic
1 shallot
1 tablespoon red wine vinegar
1 tablespoon olive oil
squeeze of lemon juice

TO SERVE
200g–300g quick cook polenta
generous knob butter
large handful grated Parmesan

1. Heat the olive oil over a high heat in a heavy-based pan. Add the lamb and sear the meat until it is browned all over, then remove from the pan and set aside.

2. Reduce the heat to medium and add the onion, garlic, rosemary, thyme, sage, celery, fennel, mushrooms and chilli flakes and sauté until the onion is soft and starting to caramelise.

3. Return the lamb to the pan, then add the tomatoes, white wine, stock and redcurrant jelly. Reduce the heat to low and simmer for at least 2 hours (the longer the better). You can also just pop it into a very low oven if that's easier.

4. While the ragù is cooking, make the chimichurri. Put all the ingredients into a food processor and blitz (or you can finely chop by hand and stir together until combined).

5. When you are ready to serve, prepare the polenta according to the instructions on the packet – we suggest also adding lots of butter and Parmesan to make it deliciously luxurious. Serve the polenta in warmed bowls and spoon the ragù on top. Grate over some more Parmesan and drizzle with the chimichurri.

Meat
and Fish

The recipes in this chapter celebrate the fantastic produce on offer to us.

We both have strong ties to farming, so the welfare of animals is something that is hugely important to us. In a world in which the industrial farming of livestock has proliferated over recent years, it seems to us more crucial than ever to only eat meat and dairy that is produced on smaller, more sustainable, kinder farms – like the one on which Lucy grew up. Billions of animals today spend their lives crammed in dark, horrible sheds. This is not farming. Pigs – inquisitive, charismatic and social as they are – suffer in particular. There is no happier sight than a family of pigs (like the ones raised by Jemima in Somerset) in an open field or woodland, the sunshine on their backs, their highly sensitive noses furrowing the cool earth looking for delicious things to eat. For us there is no alternative, so we only buy free-range meat, eggs and dairy.

It has taken us less than two generations to decimate life in the oceans, too. The seas once teemed with fish, but many species are declining rapidly. The good news is that nature recovers very quickly, given some protection. More and more countries around the world are setting aside and protecting important fish-breeding areas, and putting in place sound fisheries management rules. In those places fish stocks are bouncing back. Guides such as Fish To Fork are hugely helpful when it comes to choosing which kinds of fish to eat and which to avoid.

We love cooking with quality meat and fish, and the recipes in this chapter celebrate the fantastic produce on offer to us.

Grilled Red Mullet and Fresh Coconut Salad

Salmon Sashimi Bowl

Spiced Prawn Burgers

Crispy, Herby and Lemony Fishcakes

Summer Squid Stew

Sea Bass en Papillote

Smoked Fish with Fennel, Tarragon and Crispy Sage

Clam Linguine

Seared Tuna Carpaccio

Marinated Salmon

Chicken Burgers

Ricotta and Tarragon Stuffed Roast Chicken

Crispy Chicken

Partridge with Ras el Hanout

Spiced Quail

Spiced Yoghurt Marindted Chicken

Flattened Griddled Lamb Chops

Marinated Lamb

Lamb Koftas

Pork Tenderloin with Fennel and Honey

Grilled Red Mullet and Fresh Coconut Salad

Red mullet is a very pretty fish, especially when raw, as it has a strikingly bright pink, shimmery skin. It reminds us of the Mediterranean as it is abundant there, commonly caught off the coasts of Spain, Italy and France. It's lovely simply roasted in the oven with full summer flavours and served with sweet tomatoes.

However, this dish is not inspired by our European neighbours, but instead by the white sands and turquoise seas of Sri Lanka. It is quite possibly the best fish dish we had out there. We found a deserted beach on the south coast where the sand was so fine it almost felt like silk underfoot. The only other occupants on the beach were the fishermen in the mornings, school boys in the afternoon playing cricket and cows by night. There was also one beach shack, run by one of the wives of the fishermen. There was no menu, just whatever the daily catch was and what she felt like making. We had a fresh, zingy and absolutely delicious fried ginger and garlic mullet. The best part of all was the caramelised bits, which she piled on top of the fish, serving it with a freshly grated coconut salad and a cold beer.

Serves 4

4 whole red mullet, gutted and cleaned
1–2 tablespoons olive oil
1 tablespoon coconut oil
juice of 1 lime
small bunch of coriander
1 red chilli, finely sliced
lime wedges, to serve

FOR THE MARINADE
4 cloves garlic, chopped
large thumb-sized piece of fresh ginger, peeled and chopped
½ onion, chopped

FOR THE SALAD
1 coconut, smashed and grated
1 green chilli, finely chopped
large handful of spinach, finely sliced
1 lime, zest and juice
salt and pepper

1. Mix together all the marinade ingredients and place inside the cavity of each fish.

2. Rub the fish all over with some olive oil then put into a dish and leave to marinate in the fridge for at least half an hour, the longer the better. Meanwhile, toss all the salad ingredients together in a bowl.

3. Heat a good tablespoon of coconut oil in a large frying pan over a high heat, then add the fish and the marinade and cook in the sizzling pan for about 2 minutes. Turn over and cook for another 2 minutes; keep moving the onion mix so it doesn't burn.

4. Serve on a plate, spooning over anything that has been left in the pan, then drizzle with lime juice and sprinkle with coriander leaves and red chilli. Serve with the coconut salad and lime wedges.

Salmon Sashimi Bowl
with Pickled Cucumber, Yuzu and Brown Rice

This is a clean dish, the kind of food we could eat every day for lunch. It's fresh, with bright crisp flavours, added creaminess from the avocado, nuttiness from the brown rice and a zing from the citrus – yuzu is a Japanese citrus fruit, and you can buy the juice in the world foods aisle of most supermarkets.

Rice bowls are a typical lunch in Japan, and we love the regimented order of Japanese bento boxes, with everything served separately. That is how we like to serve this – every element has its own bowl, with colours and tastes separated so you can choose your own quantities.

We have a fantastic local fishmonger, and we often swap the fish to whatever fresh delivery he has had that day – this is wonderful with sea bass, though with that we would usually ditch the rice and add a crunchy green instead.

Serves 2

½ cucumber
½ large red chilli, sliced
6 radishes, quartered
1 teaspoon nigella seeds
2 tablespoons rice wine vinegar
1 teaspoon sugar
½ avocado, stone removed, peeled and diced
200g sushi-grade salmon, cut into 1.5cm cubes
1 teaspoon toasted sesame seeds

FOR THE DRESSING
2 teaspoons toasted sesame oil
1 tablespoon soy sauce
1 red chilli, deseeded and finely chopped
1 tablespoon mirin
1 tablespoon yuzu juice (or use lime juice)
1 lime, zested
1 tablespoon rice wine vinegar
½ tablespoon clear mild honey
2.5cm piece of fresh ginger, peeled and finely chopped
1 spring onion, finely chopped
small handful of coriander leaves

TO SERVE
150g brown rice
pickled ginger
lime wedges

1. Cook the rice according to the packet instructions, then put in a bowl and set aside.
2. Slice the cucumber lengthways on a mandoline (or with a knife) into long, thin strips and place in a bowl, then add the chilli, radishes and nigella seeds. Mix together the vinegar and sugar until the sugar dissolves, pour over the cucumber salad, toss and place in a pretty bowl; set aside.
3. Mix all the dressing ingredients together in a small jug.
4. Place the chopped avocado on a small plate or bowl, then arrange the salmon on top. Pour over the dressing and gently toss before sprinkling over the sesame seeds. Serve with the cooked brown rice, the cucumber salad, pickled ginger and lime wedges.

Spiced Prawn Burgers
with a Spinach Sauce

This burger is a nice little number – a fun one, too. Prawns are perfect for this dish as they are sweet and meaty with a good texture to them. We originally made the burger with cod but we found it too soft – you want it to have some bite.

Serves 4

400g raw tiger prawns, patted dry with kitchen paper and roughly chopped

6 spring onions, finely chopped

5cm piece of fresh ginger, peeled and finely grated

2 cloves garlic, grated

1 green chilli, finely chopped

4 limes, zested

1 teaspoon garam masala

small bunch of coriander, stalks finely chopped, leaves left whole

salt

groundnut oil, for frying

FOR THE SAUCE

splash of olive oil

1 onion, finely chopped

1 teaspoon cumin seeds

5cm piece of fresh ginger, peeled and finely chopped

2 cloves garlic, finely chopped

1 teaspoon ground turmeric

1 teaspoon garam masala

1 teaspoon cayenne pepper

3 big sweet tomatoes, chopped

squeeze of honey

200g baby spinach

100ml chicken or vegetable stock

2 tablespoons crème fraîche

1 lime, zested, plus juice for serving

small bunch of mint, leaves chopped

1. First make the sauce. Heat the oil in a pan and sauté the onion, cumin seeds, ginger and garlic until softened. Add the turmeric, garam masala and cayenne and cook over a medium heat for a minute. Add the tomatoes and honey and cook down for about 5 minutes.

2. Wash the spinach and put it into a separate pan without drying it. Put the lid on and steam over a medium heat for 3–4 minutes. Tip into a sieve and press to squeeze out all the water, then blitz coarsely in a food processor (or chop by hand).

3. Add the stock and the blitzed spinach to the pan of tomatoes and spices, then stir in the crème fraîche, lime zest and the chopped mint and reserved coriander leaves, keeping a few leaves back to garnish.

4. To make the shrimp burgers, mix all the ingredients together in a bowl until evenly combined. Form into patties, using about a handful of mixture for each one to make eight burgers.

5. Heat a little groundnut oil in a frying pan. When hot, add the cakes and fry for about 2 minutes on each side, or until crisp and golden brown. Add to the pan of green sauce and simmer for a further 5 minutes over a medium heat.

6. Serve the cakes with a squeeze of lime juice and the reserved mint and coriander leaves. This is delicious with a herby, nutty rice.

Crispy, Herby and Lemony Fishcakes
with Pea and Mint Dip

As advertised, these fishcakes are very definitely crispy, herby and lemony. Easy as pie and thank the Lord no peeling, chopping or boiling of potatoes. They are light and fresh so are ideal for lunch or supper, with something crunchy on the side. We couldn't help pairing them with peas; they just go hand in hand (think fish and chips with peas). Looks like the crunchy side you are looking for might be crispy chips…

Serves 2–3

200g skinless salmon fillet
200g skinless cod fillet
1–2 glasses (175–350ml) white wine
3 bay leaves
1 tablespoon butter or olive oil
2 leeks, finely chopped
2 cloves garlic, finely chopped
bunch of chives, finely chopped
bunch of parsley, leaves finely chopped
1 egg, beaten
1 teaspoon Dijon mustard
3 spring onions, chopped
5 tablespoons dried breadcrumbs
1 lemon, zest and juice
dried breadcrumbs and polenta, for dusting
groundnut oil, for frying

FOR THE GREEN SAUCE
100g frozen peas
100g crème fraîche
1 clove garlic
small bunch of mint, leaves picked
small bunch of dill
splash of olive oil
salt and pepper

1. First make the green sauce. Place the frozen peas in a bowl, cover with boiling water and leave for about 10 seconds, then drain and put into a food processor. Add the remaining sauce ingredients and blitz. Season with salt and pepper, then put into a bowl and chill in the fridge.

2. Place the salmon and cod into a small pan, pour over the white wine (to cover), add the bay leaves and season with salt and pepper. Cover the pan with a lid, bring to a simmer and cook for 4–5 minutes. Remove from the heat and set aside to cool with the lid off (don't worry if the fish isn't totally cooked, as it will be cooked again).

3. Heat the butter or oil in a small frying pan and add the leeks and garlic. Sauté for 5 minutes, then transfer to a bowl. Add the chives, parsley, egg, mustard, spring onions, breadcrumbs, lemon zest and juice and season with salt and pepper. Mix until combined, then flake in the fish and very carefully mix together, trying not to break up the fish too much.

4. Sprinkle a mixture of breadcrumbs and polenta onto a plate and season with salt and pepper. Take a small handful of the mixture and shape into a patty, then dip both sides into the polenta mix and put onto a plate. Repeat with the remaining mixture. Transfer to the fridge to firm up – ideally for an hour.

5. Heat the oil in a wide pan over a medium heat. Once hot, add the fishcakes in batches and cook for 1–2 minutes on each side, or until golden. Remove and drain on kitchen paper; repeat with the remaining fishcakes. Serve with the green sauce and a lovely dry white wine.

Both the fishcakes and the green sauce can be made in advance. Make the fishcakes up to the end of step 4, then cover and keep in the fridge for up to 24 hours.

Summer Squid Stew

This is a celebration of summer flavours, tastes that will transport you to balmy days, straw hats and the smell of freshly cut grass. You can almost feel the warmth. It is a fresh and happy dish and it's also an easy one, although make sure that you use good-quality ingredients. Here we are using Italian flavours – it's fine if you are in Italy and you have the best ingredients on your doorstep, but here we need to be a bit more scrupulous when sourcing the vegetables: don't pick up floury tomatoes with no flavour, but look for sweet little rubies that will make this dish sing.

Serves 6

1kg baby squid, cleaned and butterflied and tentacles reserved

2–3 tablespoons olive oil

2 small red onions, chopped

1 stick celery, finely chopped

4 cloves garlic, sliced

2 chillies, deseeded and finely chopped

2 large bay leaves

2 sprigs of thyme

1 large glass (250ml) dry white wine

4 large fresh tomatoes (approx. 500g), chopped

pinch of saffron threads (optional)

handful of pitted black olives, roughly chopped

1 heaped tablespoon capers

big pinch of chopped basil leaves

big pinch of chopped parsley leaves

squeeze of lemon juice

salt and pepper

1. Cut the squid into 5cm pieces, then lay the pieces and tentacles on kitchen paper to dry. Once dried, toss the squid in a couple of tablespoons of olive oil and season well with salt and pepper.

2. Get a frying pan very hot, then add the squid in batches, making sure the pieces have plenty of space in the pan. They should take no longer than a few minutes to crisp up.

3. Once done, leave the squid to rest to one side and add another splash of olive oil to the pan. Add the onion, celery, garlic, chillies, bay leaves and thyme. Sauté for about 5 minutes until the onions are starting to caramelise.

4. Deglaze the pan with the white wine and add the tomatoes, squid and saffron, if using. Simmer for about 30 minutes until the squid is soft and tender.

5. Add the olives, capers, chopped herbs and a good squeeze of lemon juice and serve immediately with a nice crusty bread, some aioli (see page 59) and very cold white wine.

Sea Bass en Papillote

This mess-free recipe is an impressive and entertaining little dish to make when friends come over for supper. The fun is in the individual bags that you open like a present, to be met with wonderful smells and juicy fish bursting with flavour.

1. Preheat the oven to 200°C/gas 6.

2. First make the dressing. Bash the lemon grass and lime leaves together either in a mortar and pestle or with a rolling pin, until the juices are released and it begins to become mushy. Add to a bowl with the remaining dressing ingredients and stir to combine.

3. Get two large pieces of baking paper and place each one over a cereal bowl, then press them down to make a well in each. Divide the spinach and courgette between the two sheets of paper and place a sea bass fillet on top (if a little on the long side cut into two pieces). Next pour the dressing over each fillet and finish with the coriander and few slices of lime. Bring the tops of the paper together at the top and then tie with string.

4. Place both parcels on a baking tray and cook in the oven for 20–25 minutes. Serve hot with steamed jasmine rice and extra chopped red chillies if you like it hot (like us!).

Serves 2

large handful of spinach, washed

1 courgette, thinly sliced into rounds

2 wild sea bass fillets

small bunch of coriander

1 lime, cut into wedges

FOR THE DRESSING

1 lemon grass stalk, roughly chopped

4 lime leaves

1 shallot, finely diced

1 red chilli, finely chopped (deseed if you prefer less heat), plus extra to serve (optional)

5cm piece of fresh ginger, peeled and cut into very thin matchsticks

1 large clove garlic, thinly sliced

1 tablespoon soy sauce

1 tablespoon mirin

1 tablespoon toasted sesame oil

1 teaspoon sugar or honey

1 teaspoon fish sauce

1 lime, zest and juice

Smoked Fish with Fennel, Tarragon and Crispy Sage

This is a very, very good dish, and an easy one at that. It is flavoursome, creamy and not too heavy and we usually serve it just like this – no need for a side dish – although you might want some warm, crusty bread for mopping up the plates. We sometimes serve it with a poached egg on top.

1. Heat the butter or oil in a pan over a medium heat and add the leeks, garlic, fennel, bay leaves and chilli flakes and sauté for a good 5 minutes. Stir in the mustard then add the white wine and stock. Bring to a simmer.

2. Add the fish (if you are using hot-smoked salmon keep it back until later, as this is already cooked) and simmer gently for 5 minutes, or until cooked through.

3. Add the spinach and gently submerge and stir in so it wilts. Next add the crème fraîche, hot-smoked salmon, if using, lemon zest and juice and tarragon. Season to taste with salt and pepper and remove from the heat.

4. Heat the tablespoon of olive oil in a small frying pan and add the sage leaves. Fry until crisp, then drain on kitchen paper.

5. Ladle the fish into warmed bowls and scatter with the crispy sage leaves. Serve with a chunk of good bread.

Serves 4

knob of butter or a splash of olive oil, plus 1 tablespoon olive oil for the sage

2 leeks, chopped

2 cloves garlic, chopped

1 bulb fennel, thinly sliced

2 bay leaves

pinch of chilli flakes

1 tablespoon Dijon mustard

large glass (250ml) white wine

500ml chicken or vegetable stock

600g smoked fish (a mix of smoked haddock, cod or hot-smoked salmon), cut into cubes

2 large handfuls of spinach

400ml crème fraîche

1 lemon, zest and juice

bunch of tarragon, leaves chopped

handful of sage leaves

salt and pepper

4 poached eggs (see page 44), to serve (optional)

Clam Linguine
with Smoked Ham, Cider and Leeks

We are suckers for a good *linguine alle vongole* and we make it a lot, with different variations. We're sure Italians would be horrified if we were to compare this to their classic dish (sorry!) but this variation came about on a day when we were snowed under at the office and needed a quick working lunch – and it turned out to be an absolute winner. It is a beautifully balanced dish; the sweetness of the clams works very well with the smokiness of the ham, both of which are complemented by the cider.

1. Heat the olive oil and butter in a large pan over a medium heat and add the garlic and chilli flakes. Fry until just starting to turn golden, then add the leeks, shallot, fennel and ham. Continue to fry until they have cooked down and are beginning to caramelise.

2. In a separate large pan, bring the cider to a simmer and then add the clams, bathing them in the cider. Cover with a lid and cook for about 3 minutes, or until all the clams have opened, shaking the pan once or twice during this time (remove and discard any that remain closed). Once the clams have opened, take them off the heat and strain, reserving the liquid.

3. Add this cider/clam juice liquid to the leek mixture and bubble down for a few minutes, then add the clams, mustard and herbs.

4. Cook the linguine according to the packet instructions, or until al dente. Drain and add to the clams, season with salt and pepper and use tongs to toss the pasta in the sauce. Serve with lemon wedges.

Serves 4

good glug of olive oil
1 tablespoon butter
4 cloves garlic, thinly sliced
1 teaspoon chilli flakes
2 leeks, finely chopped
1 shallot, finely chopped
1 bulb fennel, finely chopped
80g smoked ham, chopped
250ml dry cider
1kg clams, soaked in fresh water for 20 minutes (discard any that do not close firmly when tapped)
1 tablespoon Dijon mustard
small bunch of mixed herbs (tarragon, chives and parsley), leaves finely chopped
200g linguine
sea salt and pepper
lemon wedges, to serve

Seared Tuna Carpaccio
with Spiced Lentils

We have been making this recipe for years – it actually came from Lucy's cookery school back in the day. It was a fantastically fun course and she came away with a bible that we both use regularly. This is one of our real favourites, so we had to include it in the book. It is a vibrant, fresh-tasting dish bursting with life and flavour, and is great as a chic little starter or a light main dish. A very good recipe indeed.

Serves 6–8

2 tablespoons soy sauce
1 tablespoon Dijon mustard
1 tablespoon honey
2 tablespoons sunflower oil
225g tuna loin (in one piece)
2–3 tablespoons Sichuan peppercorns
1 tablespoon sea salt
pinch of Chinese five spice
1 tablespoon mirin
juice of 1 lime

FOR THE LENTILS
225g Puy lentils
thumb-sized piece of fresh ginger
4 cloves garlic, 2 left whole, 2 crushed
1 red onion, finely chopped
2 long red chillies, deseeded and thinly sliced
1 teaspoon cumin seeds, roasted and crushed
½ preserved lemon, finely chopped
2 tablespoons white wine vinegar mixed with ½ tablespoon soft brown sugar
4 tablespoons soy sauce
handful of chopped coriander leaves
handful of chopped parsley leaves
handful of chopped mint leaves
salt and pepper

1. First prepare the tuna– you can do this up to 24 hours in advance. Whisk together the soy sauce, mustard and honey in a shallow dish.

2. Heat the sunflower oil in a frying pan over a high heat and sear the tuna on all sides. Transfer to the dish with the soy mix and carefully turn in the mixture; leave to cool.

3. Heat a dry heavy-based pan until smoking and add the Sichuan peppercorns; toss until they start to smell aromatic. Take off the heat and crush finely, then mix with the salt and the Chinese five spice and sprinkle over a plate. Lift the tuna out of its marinade and then roll in the spice mix. Wrap in cling film and place in the fridge until needed.

4. Whisk the mirin and lime juice into the soy sauce marinade to make a dressing and leave to one side while you make the lentil salad.

5. Bring a pan of salted water to the boil and add the lentils, ginger and whole cloves of garlic. Simmer for about 20 minutes until tender.

6. Meanwhile, mix the crushed garlic, red onion, chillies, cumin seeds, preserved lemon, vinegar and sugar and soy sauce and season with salt and pepper. Add the drained lentils (removing the ginger and cloves of garlic) while they are still warm, to soak up the flavours. Leave to cool.

7. Once the lentils are cool, stir in the herbs and then scatter them over a serving platter. Unwrap the tuna and cut as thinly as you can using a very sharp knife. Arrange carefully over the lentils. Serve the dressing on the side (the tuna is so pretty and pink that it's best to dress just before eating).

Marinated Salmon
with Lemon Grass, Ginger, Lime and Green Herbs

A fantastically easy recipe – when you taste it you wouldn't think it only took five minutes to prepare. When you first make the marinade it is a vigorous, vibrant bright green, which is quite spectacular when you pour it over the delicate pink salmon. Sadly you'll have to enjoy this moment by yourself as it turns a rather muddy green on cooking, so your guests won't enjoy such wondrous colours. All is not lost, however; the trick is to scatter the fish liberally with fresh herbs and sliced spring onions when serving. Perfect with nutty brown rice.

1. Preheat the oven to 200°C/gas 6.
2. Place the salmon, skin side down, in an ovenproof dish.
3. Roughly chop all the marinade ingredients, place in a food processor or blender and blitz until smooth. Pour over the salmon and leave to marinate in the fridge for at least 30 minutes but ideally for a few hours.
4. Transfer to the oven to cook for 15–20 minutes, or until just cooked (it's nice to have it a little pink in the middle). Transfer to a serving platter and sprinkle over the chopped spring onions and coriander leaves.

Serves 4

500g salmon fillet (in one piece), pin-boned

3–4 spring onions, finely chopped

bunch of coriander leaves

FOR THE MARINADE

1 lemon grass stalk, woody end and outer leaf removed

1 shallot

1 green chilli, stalk removed

2 tablespoons soy sauce

bunch of coriander

bunch of mint, leaves picked

2 cloves garlic

thumb-sized piece of fresh ginger, peeled

1 lime, zested, plus juice of 2

2 tablespoons rice wine vinegar

little squeeze of honey

salt and pepper

Chicken Burgers
with Maple-chipotle Mayonnaise and Pickled Cucumber

Makes about 10

700g chicken (minced or not; use a mixture of breast and thigh)

10 spring onions, finely chopped

4 tablespoons finely grated Parmesan

75g peeled and grated fresh ginger

4 cloves garlic, crushed

large bunch of coriander, stalks and leaves chopped

1½ tablespoons rice wine vinegar

3 tablespoons toasted sesame oil

1½ tablespoons soy sauce

2 limes, zest and juice

groundnut oil (or other flavourless oil), for frying

FOR THE PICKLED CUCUMBERS

2 tablespoons rice wine vinegar

1 teaspoon caster sugar

½ cucumber

1 teaspoon toasted sesame seeds

1 red chilli, sliced

FOR THE MAPLE-CHIPOTLE MAYONNAISE

6 tablespoons mayonnaise

5 chipotle peppers in adobo sauce (or 1 teaspoon smoked paprika and 1 teaspoon harissa)

1 lime, zest and juice

1 teaspoon maple syrup

salt and pepper

TO SERVE

burger buns (we like to toast them a little)

2 Little Gem lettuces, leaves separated

2 plum tomatoes, cut into 1cm slices

2 red onions, sliced into thin half-moons and fried until crisp

This burger feels fresh and different – and it's on the healthy side as far as burgers go. You could make it even lighter by ditching the bun, keeping the onions raw and enjoying it as a salad – perfect in the summer straight off the barbecue. We do love the whole fun of a burger, though, using your hands to eat and generally making a bit of a mess!

We like to mince our own meat, as it has a better texture and flavour. Do try to get hold of the chipotle in adobo sauce, too; it really takes the burger to a whole new level. You can buy it from big supermarkets or online.

1. First make the pickled cucumber. Mix the vinegar and the sugar together until it dissolves. Using a vegetable peeler, shave the cucumber lengthways, working all the way round but stopping when you get to the seeds. Pour the vinegar mixture over the cucumber strips and toss; set aside. When you are ready to serve, lightly toast the sesame seeds and scatter over the cucumber along with the chilli.

2. Make the mayo: put the mayonnaise in a blender with the chipotle peppers, lime zest and juice and maple syrup and season.

3. If you are using minced chicken then simply place in a bowl. If not, roughly chop up, removing any gristle and pop into a food processor. Pulse until it is just minced – you do not want to form a paste. Add the rest of the burger ingredients to the minced chicken, season with salt and pepper and combine. Using your hands, shape into about 10 burgers and place on a plate, then flatten slightly with your hand (you don't want them too thick as they must cook fully all the way through, unlike traditional beef burgers).

4. Heat the oil in a large frying pan over a medium–high heat. Add the chicken burgers and cook, in batches, for 4 minutes each side – they should be well seared. Remove from the pan and drain on kitchen paper (we would always check one by cutting in half to make sure they are fully cooked – do not serve pink).

5. Serve in toasted buns with lettuce, tomatoes, crispy onions, a generous dollop of the smoky mayo and the pickled cucumber on the side.

Ricotta and Tarragon Stuffed Roast Chicken

We love this way of preparing roast chicken and have numerous recipes on a theme. It's the perfect way to ensure a moist, succulent chicken that also has the wow factor. The key is to be very careful when lifting the skin of the chicken, making sure you don't tear it and pushing the stuffing as far as the legs, too. We often experiment with what we have in the fridge – you can't really go wrong as chicken is such a wonderful, versatile bird.

1. Preheat the oven to 220°C/gas 7. Remove the chicken from the fridge to bring it to room temperature.

2. Pat the chicken all over with kitchen paper to dry it, then rub inside and out with salt and pepper.

3. Mix all the stuffing ingredients together in a bowl and season with salt and pepper. Use your fingers to gently ease the skin away from the chicken, taking care not to tear it, and push the mixture under the skin. If possible, lift the skin and get the mixture down to the legs by pushing it through.

4. Put the lemon half and garlic cloves into the cavity of the chicken. Rub the chicken all over with olive oil and place in a roasting tray. Roast in the oven for about 1 hour, reducing the temperature to 180°C/gas 4 after 40 minutes. Test whether it is done by piercing the thickest part of the thigh with a sharp knife – if the juices run clear, it's cooked.

5. Remove from the oven and let the bird rest for a bit, as this will bring all the flavours together.

Serves 4

1 whole organic chicken
  (approx. 1.5kg)
½ lemon
few cloves garlic
1–2 tablespoons olive oil
salt and pepper

FOR THE STUFFING
250g ricotta
2 lemons, zested
1 tablespoon grated Parmesan
1 tablespoon chopped
  tarragon leaves
1 tablespoon chopped chives
2 spring onions, finely chopped
3 cloves garlic, crushed

Crispy Chicken
with Tomatoes, Roast Garlic Mash and Smashed Herb Oil

It's crucial to use a chicken breast with the skin on for this recipe (or a chicken supreme, which still has its bone in). We always cook chicken breasts with the skin on – it tastes so much better and helps it to stay moist (and it's secretly our favourite bit, especially on a roast).

This is a really good dish – like, really good. It sings and dances all the way to a happy place. Once you make this for a dinner party it will become a staple – just follow with something light and creamy for dessert.

Serves 2

1 whole head of garlic
2 large baking potatoes, peeled and cut into chunks
25g butter
1½ tablespoons crème fraîche
2 skin-on chicken breasts or chicken supremes
drizzle of olive oil
2 tablespoons white wine
6 tomatoes, halved
small bunch of thyme, leaves picked
pinch of sugar
drizzle of balsamic vinegar
sea salt and pepper

FOR THE BASIL OIL
small bunch of basil, leaves torn
juice of ½ lemon
50ml olive oil

1. Preheat the oven to 220°C/gas 7.

2. Slice off the top of the head of garlic and place in an ovenproof dish. Sprinkle with some water and roast in the oven for about 30 minutes until the cloves are starting to bubble out of the top. Set aside to cool.

3. Put the potatoes into a pan, cover with water, bring to the boil and simmer for about 20 minutes until soft to the touch, then drain. Mash the potato by using a potato ricer (if you don't have one, then just mash until smooth), place in a bowl and add the butter, crème fraîche and a large pinch of salt and pepper. Squeeze out the soft garlic from its skins, add to the potato and mix well.

4. Meanwhile place the tomatoes in an ovenproof dish, sprinkle with the thyme leaves and sugar, and drizzle with balsamic vinegar and olive oil. Season with salt and pepper, and place in the oven for 20–30 minutes until starting to colour. Set aside.

5. Place an ovenproof frying pan over a high heat. Rub the chicken with a drizzle of olive oil and season with salt and pepper, then place in the pan. Fry for about 4–5 minutes, skin side down, then turn and cook for another 2–3 minutes. Remove pan from heat and place in the oven for 8 minutes. Remove from the oven and leave to rest for at least 2 minutes. Meanwhile, pour the white wine into the pan and bubble for a minute or two to deglaze the pan.

6. Make the basil oil: grind all the ingredients together using a mortar and pestle until the leaves are broken up and you have a chunky green oil. Season with salt and pepper.

7. Put a good dollop of the garlic mash on a warm plate followed by three tomatoes and the chicken breast. Pour over the white wine reduction and drizzle with the basil oil.

Partridge with Ras el Hanout,
Rose Harissa, Mint Yoghurt and Fennel Salad

We love partridge. They're funny little birds – you always see them in pairs as they mate for life and trot around together (very sweet). The ones you see most these days are the red-legged partridge, but if you come across a grey-legged partridge then jump at the chance to buy it, as they are delicate and tender. Spatchcocking a small bird like this is easy to do at home, you don't have to ask the butcher to do it. We also find it easier to eat – you want to get your hands involved, making sure you nibble off every little morsel.

Serves 4

4 teaspoons ras el hanout
1 tablespoon honey
1 tablespoon rose water
3 cloves garlic, crushed
5 tablespoons olive oil
zest and juice of 1 lemon
4 partridges (or use quail or poussin and decrease or increase the cooking time respectively)
salt and pepper
flatbreads (see page 265), to serve
lime wedges, to serve

FOR THE MINT YOGHURT
200g Greek yoghurt
1 clove garlic, crushed
bunch of mint, leaves shredded

FOR THE SALAD
½ bulb fennel, very thinly sliced
½ red onion, thinly sliced
small bunch of rocket
small bunch of coriander leaves
juice of 1 lime
drizzle of olive oil

FOR THE ROSE HARISSA
1 x 400g tin chopped tomatoes
2–3 teaspoons rose harissa (or use harissa plus 2 teaspoons rosewater)
1 teaspoon honey
bunch of coriander, chopped

1. Mix together the ras el hanout, honey, rose water, garlic, olive oil, lemon zest and juice and some salt and pepper.

2. Spatchcock the partridges one at a time as follows: turn the partridge so it is breast side down. Use a good pair of scissors to cut down one side of the backbone, then cut down the other side of the backbone and remove it. Turn the partridge over and squash down the breastbone with the base of your hand until flattened. Place all the partridges in a shallow dish, pour the marinade over the birds and rub in. Cover and refrigerate, ideally for a few hours.

3. Mix all the yoghurt ingredients together and put into a small serving bowl. Combine the fennel, red onion, rocket and coriander to make the salad and then dress with the lime juice and olive oil. Place in a pretty bowl ready to serve.

4. Put the chopped tomatoes, rose harissa (or harissa and rosewater) into a pan and bring to the boil. Reduce the heat and simmer for about 10 minutes to reduce, then add the honey and chopped coriander. Season with salt and pepper, then remove from the heat and put into a serving bowl.

5. When you are ready to cook, preheat the oven to 220°C/gas 7.

6. Place a frying pan over a high heat until smoking, then add the partridges and sear for a couple of minutes on both sides until browned. Transfer to a roasting tray and pop into the hot oven for 20–25 minutes. Take out and rest for a good 10–15 minutes.

7. Place the birds on a serving board. Serve with the two sauces, the salad, flatbreads and lime wedges (it's also very good with couscous to soak up the juices).

Spiced Quail
with Saffron and Preserved Lemon

This is a great little number to make for a dinner party, as it feels special and different with its spices and preserved lemon. It's good all year round, as it's easy enough to order quails from your local butcher. The dish was inspired by a favourite River Café recipe that uses rosemary and red wine, but we gave it an exciting Middle Eastern vibe, which complements these birds. They soak up all the flavours, making them succulent and tender.

Serves 2–4

4 quails (or poussin)

splash of olive oil

1 red onion, chopped

2 sprigs of thyme, leaves picked and roughly chopped

1 bulb fennel, thinly sliced

1 stick celery, finely chopped

2 cloves garlic, finely chopped

1 tablespoon fennel seeds

1 red chilli, deseeded and chopped

glass (175ml) of vermouth (or use Pernod or a dry white wine)

1 heaped teaspoon smoked paprika

1 large preserved lemon (or 2 small), chopped

250ml chicken or vegetable stock

1 x 400g tin chopped tomatoes

squeeze of honey

1 tablespoon chopped tarragon leaves

small bunch of parsley, leaves chopped

salt and pepper

1. Remove the quails from the fridge and remove from any packaging to let them come to room temperature and dry out before cooking. Season well all over.

2. Heat the oil in a frying pan and sear the quails all over until golden brown. You might need to do this in batches. Remove from the pan and set aside.

3. In the same pan, sauté the onion, thyme, fennel, celery, garlic, fennel seeds and chilli over a medium heat for 5–8 minutes, or until the onion is soft and translucent. Keep stirring. Pour in the vermouth and let it catch all the edges and reduce into the pan for a minute. Add the paprika, preserved lemon, stock and tomatoes, reduce the heat and simmer for 15 minutes.

4. Return the quails to the pan and add the honey. Put the lid on and cook for a further 5 minutes, then stir in the tarragon and parsley. This is delicious served with a lemony fennel and rocket salad, buttery polenta and a spiced yoghurt (see page 257).

Spiced Yoghurt Marinated Chicken

We use this marinade a lot – on a whole bird like this one, on a spatchcocked chicken on the barbecue in summer, or simply on chicken thighs, which work well in the oven or on the barbecue. The magic of marinating chicken in yoghurt is that it tenderises it; the active bacteria in the yoghurt breaks down protein, making your chicken succulent and moist. You can play around with the marinade, changing up the spices by adding smoked paprika, cumin or coriander, or drop the spices altogether and make it herby.

1. Mix the yoghurt, garlic, spices, lime zest and juice and honey together and pour over the chicken, making sure the whole thing is coated. Marinade for at least 2 hours, ideally overnight, turning occasionally to make sure the chicken is coated in the marinade.

2. Preheat the oven to 220°C/gas 7.

3. Remove the chicken from the fridge and place in an ovenproof dish, loosely covered with foil. Place in the oven and cook for 45 minutes, then remove the foil. Cook for a further 30 minutes until nicely golden and cooked through (the juices should run clear when the thickest part of the thigh is pierced with a skewer). If you are cooking chicken thighs, the total cooking time will be less – about 30–40 minutes. Remove the foil for the last 15 minutes of cooking.

4. Leave to rest for 15 minutes before serving with a crunchy salad and some rice or potatoes.

Serves 4–6

6 tablespoons natural or Greek yoghurt

3 cloves garlic, crushed

4 teaspoons garam masala

1–2 teaspoons chilli powder

2 teaspoons ground cinnamon

1 lime, zest and juice

2 tablespoons honey

1 whole chicken (approx. 1.5kg) or 6 skin-on chicken thighs

Flattened Griddled Lamb Chops
with Rosemary Borlotti Beans and Wilted Spinach

This is a brilliant dish that reminds us of summertime – the smells as it cooks will transport you to holidays spent eating outside. Ideally we like to use fresh borlotti beans, but these can only be sourced during summer – if you are lucky enough to find fresh ones, they don't need to be pre-soaked. We've included the method for dried beans in this recipe, so that it can be made all year round. They still taste delicious; they just need a little extra attention. You will need to soak them in cold water for at least six hours (ideally overnight) to plump them up. If you are in a rush then use good-quality tinned ones – that would make this a very fast dinner (on the table in 15 minutes), as they don't need to be cooked, simply warmed through with the other ingredients.

Serves 2

6 lamb cutlets, fat trimmed

olive oil

3 sprigs of rosemary, keep 2 whole and finely chop the leaves of 1

1 teaspoon fennel seeds

150g borlotti beans, soaked for 6 hours at least and drained

1 whole head of garlic

1 onion, finely chopped

2 bay leaves

1 plum tomato, halved

few sprigs of sage

1 lemon, zested, plus juice of ½

1 teaspoon chilli flakes

1 clove garlic, sliced

4 drained anchovies

large handful of baby leaf spinach

1 tablespoon chopped parsley leaves

salt and pepper

lemon wedges, to serve

1. Place the chops on a wooden board. Using the end of a rolling pin, gently beat the meat to about half its original thickness, keeping the bones intact. Put the chops into a shallow bowl, season generously, drizzle with olive oil and massage in the chopped rosemary and fennel seeds.

2. Put the soaked and drained beans into a pan and add fresh cold water to cover by a couple of centimetres. Add the whole garlic head, chopped onion, bay leaves and tomato. Add a few glugs of olive oil and the sage and whole rosemary sprigs.

3. Simmer for 45–60 minutes with the lid on, then turn off the heat and season well with salt. Add the lemon zest and juice and let sit for 10 minutes to soak up the seasoning. We like to keep the bean mixture loose, so add extra water to your liking.

4. Place a griddle pan over a high heat until smoking hot and add the lamb chops. Griddle to your liking – we like a minute or so on each side – pressing down as you cook.

5. In a separate pan, heat a generous amount (about 2 tablespoons) of olive oil and add the chilli flakes, sliced garlic and anchovies. Cook until the anchovies break up, then take off the heat and add the spinach and chopped parsley; stir until wilted.

6. Toss the spinach and parsley mixture through your beans and serve with the griddled lamb on top and lemon wedges for squeezing over.

Marinated Lamb
with Baba Ganoush and Sweet Tomatoes

We have quite a weakness for Middle Eastern food. It has to do with the combination of flavours, textures and colours – they just get it right. This is when cooking gets inventive and exciting; choosing which spices to pair together, adding fresh sharp tones from herbs, the cooling effect of yoghurt mixtures and well-thought-out marinades – it's inventive cooking that isn't fussy, just good, honest, rustic food. We love it.

Lamb neck is a fabulously underrated and inexpensive cut of lamb, with a delicious flavour, but this dish would also be good with loin.

Serves 4–6

600g good-quality lamb neck, cut into 3cm cubes

1 tablespoon groundnut oil

3 large sweet tomatoes, roughly chopped

coriander leaves, to garnish

FOR THE SPICE MIX

1 tablespoon coriander seeds

1 tablespoon cumin seeds

1 cinnamon stick

1 tablespoon fennel seeds

1 star anise

FOR THE MARINADE

bunch of mint leaves

bunch of coriander

thumb-sized piece of fresh ginger, peeled

6 cloves garlic

2 tablespoons red wine vinegar

2 tablespoons soy sauce

1 tablespoon maple syrup

juice of 2 limes

salt and pepper

FOR THE BABA GANOUSH

6 aubergines, pricked all over with a fork

1 heaped tablespoon butter

4 garlic cloves, crushed

3 tablespoons yoghurt

2 teaspoons ground coriander

1 large lemon, zest and juice

2 heaped tablespoons tahini

1. Preheat the oven to 220°C/gas 7.

2. Tip all the spices for the spice mix into a dry frying pan and toast over a medium heat until aromatic. Grind to a fine powder in a spice grinder or with a mortar and pestle.

3. Put all the marinade ingredients into a food processor with a heaped tablespoon of the spice mix (the rest can be kept in a jar to use another time). Blitz until combined (you may need to scrape down the sides of the bowl) and then tip into a bowl. Add the cubed lamb and stir to coat in the marinade. Leave for as long as possible – overnight would be ideal, but a few hours will do.

4. Place the aubergines on a tray and put in the oven. You want them to be as smoky and charred as possible – keep them in there for up to 1 hour, turning every 15 minutes. The moment they blacken, take them out and leave to cool. Once cool, slice them open and scoop out the flesh, then place into a colander set over a sink and let the liquid drain out.

5. Heat the butter in a frying pan over a medium heat and add the garlic. Once golden, add the yoghurt, ground coriander, lemon zest and juice. Mix together, then add the aubergine and tahini and season to taste.

6. When you are ready to cook, place a frying pan over a high heat and add the groundnut oil; just before it starts smoking, add the lamb. Cook in batches for about 4–5 minutes, getting the outsides seared and crisp, but leaving it rare inside.

7. To serve, spread the baba ganoush on a serving plate, leaving a gap in the middle. Put the lamb into the middle and pour over any remaining liquid from the pan. Place the chopped tomatoes around the lamb and garnish with coriander leaves.

Lamb Koftas
with Smoky Tomato Sauce and Mint Yoghurt

Koftas are essentially meatballs. There are hundreds of variations of meatball all over the world. They can be steamed, fried, poached, baked, grilled or marinated, made of any sort of meat and in India they are often made with potato or paneer. We love the Greek way of serving them with tzatziki, or having them in Morocco in a tagine, or in Italy with a simple tomato sauce. Whichever way you serve them, make sure you have some sort of delicious sauce, and bread for dipping, wrapping or stuffing.

Our favourite kofta is lamb and we use the leg, which cooks well over a high heat so it is crisp on the outside and pink in the middle. You can also use leftover lamb for this recipe, especially if it has been on the barbecue. We like to grind our own meat in a food processor as we like the texture, but bought mince is fine too. Either way, these little meatballs are juicy and fresh and very moreish. If you don't have time to make the tomato sauce then serve in a flatbread with the garlic yoghurt and lots of herbs.

Serves 4–6

400g lamb leg meat (or a mix of shoulder and leg is good too)
1 onion, roughly chopped
2 cloves garlic, crushed
bunch of coriander, leaves chopped
bunch of mint, leaves picked and chopped
bunch of parsley, leaves chopped
2 teaspoons ground cinnamon
2 teaspoons ground cumin
2 teaspoons ground coriander
2 teaspoons salt
1–2 eggs
groundnut oil, for frying
coriander leaves, to garnish

FOR THE SAUCE
splash of olive oil
1 onion, finely chopped
2 cloves garlic, finely chopped
1 x 400g tin chopped tomatoes
2 teaspoons harissa
1 teaspoon sugar
salt and pepper

FOR THE YOGHURT
150g Greek yoghurt
1 clove garlic, crushed
juice of ½ lemon
bunch of mint, leaves chopped

1. If you are mincing your own meat, pulse the lamb in a food processor until it is the texture of mince. Transfer to a large bowl.

2. Add the onion, garlic, herbs, ground spices and salt to the lamb and use your hands to combine. Beat the eggs and add to the lamb a little at a time, combining with your hands until it all comes together.

3. Roll tablespoons of the mixture into rounds and place on a plate. Put in the fridge for 30 minutes–1 hour to let the flavours come together.

4. Make the tomato sauce. Heat the oil in a pan over a medium heat and add the onion and garlic. Cook for a few minutes, then add the tomatoes, harissa and sugar and season. Simmer for 10–15 minutes. Make the yoghurt by mixing all the ingredients together in a bowl.

5. Take the koftas out the fridge. Place a large frying pan over a high heat and add some groundnut oil. Add the koftas and fry on all sides until golden, then remove from the pan and drain on kitchen paper.

6. Pour the tomato sauce into an ovenproof dish and scatter the koftas over it. If you are ready to eat, serve right away with a drizzle of yoghurt and some torn coriander leaves. If you are making in advance, leave to one side to cool, then reheat in an oven preheated to 180°C/gas 4 for about 20 minutes, or until warmed through.

Pork Tenderloin
with Fennel and Honey
with an Apple and Fennel Slaw

Tenderloin is a very lean cut, and this is a quick, easy and healthy dish for those weekday nights when you also want something slightly special. This is why we love pork tenderloin – the words 'quick' and 'easy' are music to our ears. Ideally you should marinate this the night before so it is all prepped – you can also chop the slaw (not the apple) and make the dressing so that once home, the whole thing is ready in less than 30 minutes.

Healthy, crunchy slaws have come a long way since our school days (Monday lunch of jacket potato and coleslaw is surely the cruelest way to start a week), but a good fresh slaw is delightful: crunchy, refreshing, light and acidic. There are no rules; just include three ingredients (here we are using cabbage, fennel and apple), followed by an onion, a handful of herbs, an oil and a citrus or a vinegar. Shred it up and there you go. Slaws are great with both meat and fish and brilliant with a barbecue, adding both crunch and colour to a spread.

Serves 3–4

3 cloves garlic

2 sprigs of rosemary, leaves picked

1½ teaspoons fennel seeds

1 teaspoon ground coriander

1 tablespoon honey

2 tablespoons cider vinegar

2 tablespoons olive oil

1 large pork tenderloin (500g), or 2 small, trimmed

FOR THE SLAW

½ cabbage, thinly sliced

1 red onion, halved and thinly sliced

2 apples, grated

large thumb-sized piece of fresh ginger, peeled and grated

1 bulb fennel, shredded

bunch of mint, leaves shredded

50g pumpkin seeds, lightly toasted

FOR THE DRESSING

3 tablespoons olive oil

2 tablespoons cider vinegar

2 tablespoons Greek yoghurt (optional)

1 tablespoon honey

1 clove garlic, crushed

juice of 1 lime

salt and pepper

1. Put the garlic, rosemary, fennel seeds, ground coriander, honey, vinegar and oil into a mini food processor and blitz until combined (or chop finely and bash together using a mortar and pestle).

2. Put the pork into a shallow dish, rub the marinade all over, then cover and refrigerate for a couple of hours.

3. Meanwhile, mix together the slaw ingredients in a bowl. Whisk the dressing ingredients together, then toss with the vegetables.

4. Preheat the oven to 220°C/gas 4 and line a baking tray with foil (to make washing-up easier). Remove the pork from the fridge to bring up to room temperature.

5. Place a wide frying pan over a high heat and sear the pork tenderloin for a couple of moments on each side, then transfer to the prepared baking tray and pour over any remaining marinade.

6. Cook for about 10 minutes (it can still be slightly pink in the middle). Leave to rest for 10–20 minutes (depending on size), slice up and serve with the cooking juices poured over and the apple and fennel slaw.

Desserts and
Sweet Things

We all deserve a little treat every now and then, so let yourself off the hook and make something you really want.

We both love a good dessert. Lucy's favourites are more along the lines of something chocolatey or caramel-y (even better if they are both together!) whereas Jemima prefers something fresher and fruitier. Either way, it needs to be a proper pudding – if you are going to have it then go the whole hog and have something decadent and delicious, none of this avocado-pretending-to-be-a-chocolate-dessert kind of thing. We all deserve a little treat every now and then, so let yourself off the hook and make something you really want – and when you have, sit back and fully enjoy it.

We like to make easy, get-ahead desserts so that there's no last-minute panic after dinner, so that if cooking for friends it is something done and out of the way. The king of these get-ahead desserts is ice cream, which never fails to impress when homemade and can be done and dusted well in advance.

When serving desserts, we try to do so in a delicate way, making even the simplest dishes an elegant end to a meal. A thin slice of chocolate cake is much more appetising than a thick wedge, and if you serve it with a little dollop of crème fraiche and some pink rose petals it will be a joy to eat. Rose petals and edible flowers are very useful for perking up desserts, but just be careful that they have not been sprayed – best of all is if you have any in the garden. We grow our own edible flowers for decoration: roses, primroses, violets and pansies are very pretty in desserts, nasturtium flowers are peppery and are lovely in salads, and borage flowers work nicely for decoration in cocktails.

Ice Cream

Vanilla Bean Yoghurt Panna Cotta

Brown Sugar and Hazelnut Meringues

Rosé Champagne and Honey Jellies

Cardamom and Orange Rice Pudding

White Chocolate, Cardamom and Raspberry Tart

Chocolate and Hazelnut Fudge Cake

Chocolate and Salted Dulce de Leche Tart

Rhubarb Banana Cake

White Chocolate, Macadamia Nut and Oat Cookies

Rhubarb and Honey Creams

Rose and Vanilla Cupcakes

Peanut Butter Cups

Three Nut Coconut Bites

Ice Cream

Long after childhood has passed, the sound of an ice cream van arriving remains an exciting, happy one. And today, proper ice cream, made from natural ingredients and not overloaded with sugar, has had an exciting revival. You can add a huge variety of flavours, textures and punchy colours to your ice cream base. Crunchiness from roasted salted nuts, purées of seasonal fruits and berries, naughty caramel swirls. We use a bit of a cheat base, which cuts out the faff of making a time-consuming custard: it is the Ben & Jerry's method of whisking eggs and sugar until pale, smooth and fluffy and then mixing in cream, milk and good quality vanilla beans. Super easy! Buying an ice cream maker is worth every penny too.

Strawberry, Basil and Mascarpone

This is a wonderful summer ice cream. It is terribly important to use flavoursome strawberries, as this ice cream won't work with imported tasteless supermarket strawberries over the winter months. If you can't find good fresh berries then use frozen. The mascarpone makes it wonderfully creamy, almost cheesecake-like. The basil gives it a complex, fresh taste, but it does make it feel slightly savoury so if making for children then you can miss that out.

Serves 6

250g mascarpone

200ml double cream

100ml whole milk

50g basil leaves, plus a few leaves to decorate

1 vanilla pod, split in half and seeds scraped out

600g strawberries, hulled

100g caster sugar

2 large eggs

good-quality balsamic vinegar, to serve (optional)

1. Put the mascarpone, cream and milk into a pan, add the basil and vanilla seeds and bring just to a simmer. Take off the heat and leave to infuse for 1 hour.

2. Put the hulled strawberries into a pan with 30g of the sugar, place over a medium heat and cook for 10 minutes. Take off the heat, allow to cool, then place in a food processor and blitz to a purée.

3. Put the eggs and remaining sugar into a large bowl and whisk until light and fluffy. Set a sieve over the bowl and pour the cream mixture into it; discard the basil leaves. Add the blitzed strawberries and stir to combine.

4. Pour the ice cream mixture into an ice cream machine and churn according to the manufacturer's instructions. When done, transfer the ice cream to a freezerproof container, cover and freeze until needed.

5. Serve with basil leaves and a splash of good-quality balsamic vinegar, if liked.

Roasted Hazelnut with Chocolate Splinters

Serves 6

2 large eggs

70g soft light brown sugar

400ml double cream

240ml whole milk

2 tablespoons liquid glucose (if you don't have any, add an extra tablespoon of sugar)

1 vanilla pod, split in half and seeds scraped out

170g toasted hazelnuts

1 teaspoon sea salt, plus extra for sprinkling

150g dark chocolate (70% cocoa solids)

1. Using a hand-held electric whisk, whisk the eggs and sugar together until light and fluffy. Add the cream, milk, glucose, if using, and vanilla seeds and combine.

2. Blitz 100g of the nuts with the sea salt in a food processor until they form a smooth paste, then mix into the ice cream mixture. Roughly chop the remaining nuts and set aside.

3. Pour the ice cream mixture into an ice cream machine and churn according to the manufacturer's instructions.

4. Meanwhile, break the chocolate into pieces and put into a heatproof bowl. Melt the chocolate by setting the bowl over a pan of just simmering water, making sure the bottom of the bowl doesn't touch the water. Once melted, take off the heat.

5. Just before your ice cream starts to set in the machine (when it is beginning to firm up), slowly pour the melted chocolate into the machine so it starts to splinter as it hardens. Do this nice and slowly – it can take about 10 minutes.

6. Once done, scoop the ice cream into a freezerproof container. Scatter the remaining chopped hazelnuts and a little sea salt over the top. Keep in the freezer for up to 2 weeks; take out about 10 minutes before serving to make scooping easier.

Extra Virgin Olive Oil

This is an interesting and superb ice cream. You wouldn't necessarily think it would work but it does, fantastically well. A sophisticated way to finish a dinner party.

Serves 6

2 large eggs

80g caster sugar

235ml whole milk

480ml double cream

1 vanilla pod, split in half and seeds scraped out

good pinch of sea salt, plus extra to serve

75ml extra virgin olive oil, plus extra to serve

1. Using a hand-held electric whisk, whisk the eggs and sugar together until light and fluffy. Add the milk, cream, vanilla seeds and salt and whisk until well combined.

2. Pour into your ice cream machine and churn according to the manufacturer's instructions. When the mixture starts to firm up, start to slowly pour in the olive oil.

3. Transfer to a plastic freezerproof container, cover and freeze until needed. Remove from the freezer a few minutes before serving to make scooping easier. This is delicious served with a drizzle of olive oil and a little sea salt.

Daim Bar and Roasted Almond

This is an absolutely delicious ice cream. All thanks to Jemima's mum, who has been making it throughout the summer for years at their house in the South of France.

As the basis for this ice cream is essentially vanilla, it is imperative that you use very good vanilla extract, or the seeds from a vanilla pod. If you want something nuttier, it is also amazing as more of an almond ice cream – add an extra 200g to the tray when roasting the nuts in stage 1 then blitz that 200g in a food processor for 5 minutes to make a nut butter. Add the nut butter into the ice cream at stage 4.

1. Preheat the oven to 220°C/gas 7. Scatter the almonds onto a baking tray and roast for about 5 minutes until toasted and golden. Remove from the oven, roughly chop and set aside.

2. Using a sharp knife, chop the Daim bars into roughly 1cm chunks. Put them into a bowl, cover and freeze.

3. Using a hand-held electric whisk, whisk the eggs and sugar together for up to 3 minutes, or until fluffy. Then carefully stir in the milk, cream, glucose, if using, and vanilla seeds. Transfer the mixture to an ice cream machine and freeze according to the manufacturer's instructions.

4. When the ice cream begins to stiffen (this happens pretty quickly) add the frozen chopped Daim bars and most of the chopped almonds with a pinch of sea salt; continue to churn.

5. Transfer the ice cream to a freezerproof container, and sprinkle over the remaining chopped almonds. Cover and freeze until needed.

Serves 6

100g almonds

3 Daim bars

2 large eggs

70g caster sugar

240ml whole milk

400ml double cream

3 tablespoons liquid glucose (if you don't have any, add an extra tablespoon of sugar)

1 vanilla pod, split in half and seeds scraped out

pinch of sea salt

Vanilla Bean Yoghurt Panna Cotta
with Poached Lavender Apricots

We love this beautiful and elegant dessert – it feels so light and clean. It is one of those brilliant dishes that you can prepare the day before, and will certainly deliver the wow factor for your guests. The clean tartness of the yoghurt in the panna cotta is just perfect with the lavender poached apricot (but don't get too over-excited with the lavender as it is easy to end up tasting like soap). The fresh apricot season in summer is sadly quite short, so if you can't get your hands on them, we are big fans of using poached rhubarb or poached plums (see page 32), especially at Christmas.

Makes 4

2 gelatine leaves
140ml double cream
50g caster sugar
1 vanilla pod, split in half and
  seeds scraped out
300g natural yoghurt

FOR THE APRICOTS
4 apricots, halved and stoned
500ml white wine
2 tablespoons caster sugar
1 lemon, peel pared, and
  juice of ½
2 teaspoons lavender (dried
  or fresh)

1. Put the gelatine leaves into a bowl and cover with some cold water. Soak until soft, about 5 minutes.

2. Gently heat the cream and sugar in a pan over a low heat. Add the vanilla seeds and pod to the pan. Bring to a simmer, stirring to help the sugar dissolve. Remove from the heat.

3. Lift the gelatine sheets from the bowl and squeeze out the water, then stir into the hot cream mixture. Once dissolved, strain into a bowl through a sieve and whisk in the yoghurt. Pour into small ramekins or pretty bowls and put into the fridge until set, up to 2 hours.

4. To poach the apricots, put them into a small pan and pour over the white wine. Place over a medium–low heat and bring to just below a simmer. Add the sugar, lemon rind and juice and poach for 10–15 minutes, turning the apricot halves once. You want them to be tender, but still keeping their form and not falling apart. Remove and place in a bowl, keeping the liquid in the pan. Add the lavender to the pan and bubble over a medium heat for 5 minutes to reduce, then strain the liquid over the apricots.

5. Serve the set panna cottas in their ramekins or bowls with the apricot halves on top and a good spoon of the poaching liquid drizzled over.

Brown Sugar and Hazelnut Meringues
with Champagne Poached Pears

We have tried making meringues with other nuts, but roasted hazelnuts really are our preference. We love keeping the hazelnuts quite chunky and the centre of the meringue chewy. The hazelnut meringue and poached pears go very well together – both are almost toffee-like. Each can also hold its own as a dessert, served simply with a dollop of crème fraîche. This is a good dessert for a party, as you can make it well in advance.

Serves 10

FOR THE PEARS
600ml Champagne or white wine
50g caster sugar
1 vanilla pod, split in half
juice of 1 lemon
5 pears, peeled and halved

FOR THE HAZELNUT
MERINGUE
3 egg whites
150g soft brown sugar or
  caster sugar
100g roasted hazelnuts,
  coarsely chopped
100g dark chocolate,
  roughly chopped

cream or crème fraîche, to serve

1. First make the pears. Preheat the oven to 180°C/gas 4.

2. Pour the champagne into a pan with the sugar and the vanilla pod and simmer until the sugar has dissolved, then add the lemon juice.

3. Place the pears cut side up in an ovenproof dish and pour the champagne mixture over. Bake in the oven for 30–40 minutes until the pears are tender. Take out and set aside to cool. You can either serve them like this, or if you have the time, pour the poaching liquid into a small pan and reduce by half to make a syrup.

4. Next make the meringue. Preheat the oven to 120°C/gas ½ and line a couple of baking sheets with baking paper.

5. Put the egg whites into a large, clean bowl and whisk with an electric whisk to form stiff peaks. Spoon by spoon, add the caster sugar (the slower the better) to create a shiny, thick meringue mixture. When all the sugar has been incorporated, add the hazelnuts and very carefully fold in with a large metal spoon.

6. Spoon 10 dessertspoon-sized blobs of meringue onto the lined baking sheets, spacing them apart. Bake for 40–60 minutes – you want the meringues to be crispy on the top but slightly soft on the bottom when pressed (you want a good chew in your meringue).

7. Once the meringues have cooled, melt the dark chocolate in a heatproof bowl set over a pan of simmering water (making sure the bottom of the bowl doesn't touch the water). Drizzle the melted chocolate over the meringues.

8. Serve on a pretty plate with a meringue, a dollop of cream or crème fraîche and a poached pear half.

When cooking for large numbers, we often double the amounts and make one huge pavlova – it never fails to impress. Just create two large circles and cook for the same amount of time. Serve with double cream softly whipped with a little icing sugar and lots of berries sprinkled over.

Rosé Champagne and Honey Jellies

This is pretty served with delicate edible flowers or rose petals in vintage glasses. It's very light, so it's a good option if you want to serve something for dessert that isn't a dense chocolate cake or something full of sugar. It's also a great recipe to keep in mind for a party, because it's very easy to multiply the recipe and you can make it days in advance. The only downside is that it will take up fridge space – not ideal if you are planning on chilling your party Champagne.

1. Simmer the water and honey together in a pan for a couple of minutes, then add the lemon zest and juice and combine. Take off the heat and add the gelatine, and stir until it has all dissolved.

2. Strain the mixture into a bowl or jug and put in the fridge. Leave in the fridge for about 1 hour until nearly set, but keep an eye on it as you don't want it setting completely just yet.

3. When it has almost set, carefully pour in the champagne and stir – try to keep as many bubbles in it as you can – then pour the mixture into your chosen serving glasses and put into the fridge to set. It will need a good couple of hours.

Serves 4–6
(depending on glass size)

250ml water

60g good-quality floral honey
(we love using heather honey
for this recipe)

1 lemon, zest and juice

12g gelatine leaves

200ml rosé Champagne or
sparkling wine

You can use cheap bubbly here, but don't use anything too sweet.
Bear in mind that the setting times will be longer if you double up
the quantities.

Cardamom and Orange Rice Pudding
with Roasted Plums

This is sophisticated yet comforting – it really is heaven in a bowl. It is lightly fragranced with orange blossom and cardamom, which work wonderfully with the caramelised, juicy roasted plums.

It is inspired by long weekend trips to Morocco, some of which took us far into the Atlas Mountains, while others were jaunts to Marrakech to pick up beautiful crockery and feast on heavily spiced tagines or warm, sticky, fruity desserts – just like this one.

Serves 4

160g pudding rice
100ml double cream
600ml whole milk
1 vanilla pod, split in half and seeds scraped out
1 teaspoon ground cardamom
1 tablespoon orange blossom water
1 tablespoon light honey

FOR THE PLUMS
4 plums, halved and stoned
1 cinnamon stick, lightly bashed
4 tablespoons orange juice
1 tablespoon soft light brown sugar

TO SERVE
yoghurt
handful of chopped pistachios (optional)

1. Preheat the oven to 200°C/gas 6 and line a small roasting dish with baking paper (to help with the washing-up).

2. First prepare the plums. Place the plums cut side up in the roasting dish and scatter the bashed cinnamon stick around the plums. Splash over the orange juice and sprinkle the brown sugar on top. Roast in the oven for 20 minutes.

3. Meanwhile, place the pudding rice in a pan with the cream, milk, vanilla seeds and cardamom. Simmer for about 20 minutes, or until the rice is cooked, then add the orange blossom water and honey. Add a little water if needed, to loosen the rice.

4. Serve the rice pudding with the roasted plums on top and a good dollop of yoghurt, sprinkled with crushed pistachios.

White Chocolate, Cardamom and Raspberry Tart
with a Pecan and Hazelnut Base

This is one of our best desserts – it might even be Jemima's favourite. It is exactly what you want in a dessert, with a crunchy nutty base, luxurious creamy centre and a tart lift from the raspberry. White chocolate and cardamom are a match made in heaven, we are always pairing them – try making white chocolate and cardamom ice cream, it's divine.

1. Preheat the oven to 180°C/gas 4. Spread both the pecans and hazelnuts out on a baking tray and roast for about 15 minutes until nicely golden. Remove and set aside to cool.

2. Place half the nuts in a food possessor and blitz to a fine powder, then put into a bowl. Blitz the rest of the nuts to a rough crumb, then mix with the powdered nuts. Add the melted butter and a pinch of sea salt and stir to combine. Tip the mixture into a 23cm loose-bottomed tart tin and press firmly up the sides and into the bottom of the tin. You want the base to be crunchy and quite thin, rather than a thick crust. Chill in the fridge while you get on with the filling.

3. Put the mascarpone, double cream, white chocolate, vanilla and cardamom into a pan and warm over a low heat, stirring all the time to let the chocolate melt, then add a pinch of salt and remove from the heat.

4. Pour the chocolate mixture into the base. Return to the fridge and leave to set for about 1 hour.

5. Put the raspberries into a sieve suspended over a bowl. Use a spoon to press the raspberries through the sieve, leaving the seeds behind in the sieve. Once done, take the nearly-set tart out of the fridge and use a teaspoon to dot blobs of the raspberry purée over the tart. Turn the teaspoon over and drag the dots a little to create a pretty, swirled effect. Return to the fridge for another 2 hours to set completely.

Serves 12

200g pecans
200g hazelnuts
175g unsalted butter, melted
2 pinches of sea salt
250g mascarpone
100ml double cream
300g good-quality white chocolate
1 teaspoon vanilla extract
1 teaspoon ground cardamom
250g raspberries

239

Chocolate and Hazelnut Fudge Cake

We have a huge number of chocolate cake recipes for all occasions, but this is top of our list. It makes a very good birthday cake, dusted with cocoa powder or icing sugar and covered in candles. It is also great for a dinner party or with an afternoon coffee. It's dense and fudgy with a slight crunch from the hazelnuts, and is always greeted with gasps of delight from guests – especially when served warm.

Serves 8–12

200g hazelnuts

250g unsalted butter, cubed, plus extra for the tin

300g good-quality dark chocolate

150g light muscovado sugar

3 tablespoons chocolate and hazelnut spread

1 teaspoon sea salt

6 eggs, separated

double cream, to serve

1. Preheat the oven to 220°C/gas 7.

2. Put the hazelnuts onto a baking tray, pop into the oven and roast for 5–10 minutes, giving the tray a good shake halfway through, until they are golden brown. Take out of the oven and leave to cool. Place into a food processor and pulse until finely chopped – if you prefer it crunchier then don't blitz to a powder.

3. Reduce the oven temperature to 180°C/gas 4. Butter a 20cm springform tin and line with baking paper.

4. Put the chocolate, butter and sugar into a pan and melt over a gentle heat – do not let the chocolate burn. Simmer gently for a couple of minutes, then take off the heat and stir in the chocolate spread and sea salt. Leave to cool.

5. Using a hand-held electric whisk, whisk the egg whites until they are fluffy, forming soft peaks. Once the chocolate mixture has cooled, beat in the egg yolks one at a time.

6. Add a couple of tablespoons of the whisked egg whites to the chocolate mixture and combine to loosen the batter, then gently fold in the remaining egg whites, followed by the hazelnuts.

7. Pour the mixture into the prepared tin and bake in the oven for 35–40 minutes. It should be dry to the touch but still slightly wobbly underneath. Leave to cool in the tin before carefully releasing and cutting into slices (the cake will most likely sink a little in the middle – this is normal!). Serve with softly whipped double cream.

Chocolate and Salted Dulce de Leche Tart

This is a Tart classic; it's from the early days of our business, and one of our favourites. Nothing can beat salty caramel, chocolate and nuts – it's the perfect combo. We still get a lot of requests for this tart – it has actually caused a considerable amount of drama in the past, with people literally fighting over the last few slices. It is a pretty indulgent dessert, so there's no pretending you are going to get skinny on this one. But sometimes you need a really naughty, indulgent, fantastic pud. You can make your own caramel, but we prefer the cheat's way of using dulce de leche, found in most supermarkets, which has a toffee-like flavour and is pretty superb.

Serves 12

100g hazelnuts
250g oat digestive biscuits
400g dark chocolate
175g unsalted butter
200ml double cream
200g dulce de leche
pinch of sea salt
vanilla ice cream, crème fraîche
   or cream, to serve

1. Preheat the oven to 220°C/gas 7.

2. Put the hazelnuts onto a baking tray, pop into the oven and roast for 5–10 minutes, giving the tray a good shake halfway through, until they are golden brown. Take out of the oven and leave to cool. Place in a food processor with the biscuits and 100g of the dark chocolate and pulse until chopped – you want a crumbly rubble, rather than a powder – then place into a bowl.

3. Melt the butter in a small pan and then pour into the hobnob mix and stir to combine. Tip the mixture into a 23cm loose-bottomed tart tin and press into the bottom and up the sides to make a crust. Chill in the fridge while you get on with the filling.

4. Put the remaining chocolate and the cream into a pan and gently melt over a low heat, stirring to make sure that nothing sticks. When just melted, take off the heat.

5. Take the biscuit base out of the fridge and spoon over the dulce de leche, using a spatula to spread out evenly. Pour over the chocolate mixture and return to the fridge.

6. After about 20 minutes, take the tart out of the fridge and sprinkle over the sea salt. Return to the fridge to set fully. Serve with vanilla ice cream, crème fraîche or cream.

Rhubarb Banana Cake

We have been cooking this for years and imagine that we will still be making it well into old age. Sometimes, if feeling naughty, we don't use rhubarb and instead hide chocolate bars in the middle. It's a favourite of our friend, the incredible photographer Tim Walker. We couldn't be happier to have one of his faves in this book, as Tart is really all down to him – he got us our first job: cooking in Houghton Hall for *Love* magazine with Kate Moss, what fun we had! Working on shoots with Tim and his team has been one of the highlights of our career catering for fashion shoots.

1. Preheat the oven to 190°C/gas 5. Butter a 20cm round springform cake tin and line with baking paper.

2. First make the rhubarb: mix the rhubarb, sugar and elderflower cordial in a small pan over a low heat and leave to soften for 20 minutes or so, stirring occasionally. Leave to cool while you make the cake.

3. Mash the bananas in a food processor, then add the sugar, butter, eggs, flour and baking powder. Whizz until well blended. Add the milk and whizz again.

4. Pour the mixture into the prepared tin, then spoon the rhubarb on top. Bake for about 50 minutes, or until a skewer inserted into the centre comes out clean. If the top is browning too much, cover it loosely with foil. Remove from the oven and leave to cool on a wire rack before releasing from the tin.

Serves 8–12

115g unsalted butter, softened, plus extra for the tin

2 very ripe bananas

170g caster sugar

3 large eggs

225g self-raising flour

1 tablespoon baking powder

2 tablespoons milk

FOR THE RHUBARB

350g rhubarb, trimmed and chopped into 3cm pieces

2 tablespoons caster sugar

1 tablespoon elderflower cordial

White Chocolate, Macadamia Nut and Oat Cookies

This is a very good cookie. We have about ten 'favourite' cookies, but this is the one that had to make it into the book. Many a time we've made these as gifts but they've never made it to the intended recipient as they are so often scoffed en route, whether it is on the train by Jemima's father or in the back of the car by Lucy's sister. Inevitably we then have to stop and pick up a very underwhelming bottle of wine or box of chocolates for our guests, who will never know that we spent the afternoon baking them such superb cookies.

1. Preheat the oven to 180°C/gas 4 and line a couple of baking sheets with baking paper.
2. Cream the butter and the sugar together until soft and pale. Add the egg, vanilla, flour and bicarbonate of soda and beat until smooth.
3. Add the oats, nuts and chocolate and fold until combined.
4. Take walnut-sized amounts of dough and place on the lined baking sheets, spacing them well apart. Bake for 10–12 minutes, then transfer to a wire rack to cool.

Makes about 20

150g unsalted butter, softened
130g light muscovado sugar
1 egg, beaten
1 teaspoon vanilla extract
50g plain flour
1 teaspoon bicarbonate of soda
130g porridge oats
100g macadamia nuts, chopped
100g white chocolate

Rhubarb and Honey Creams
with Caramelised Ginger and Pistachio

We have been obsessed with making the perfect rhubarb posset – we've made hundreds of versions of this recipe and just could not be satisfied, but knew it would be worth it in the end. It was about getting the balance right between the tartness, creaminess and sweetness. We started with how to get the rhubarb-y flavour – we boiled it, simmered it, roasted it, smashed it, squeezed it, juiced it … and in the end we found this was the best way. We wanted to make the dish without refined sugar and had many failed attempts with different honeys – we thought it would be fantastic with heather honey, but nope, that didn't work. What does work is a light honey that doesn't overpower the rhubarb. Then came the question of whether it should be served with poached rhubarb or caramelised, should we hide it at the bottom or flaunt it on the top … and finally how should we get the crunch. Just as we nearly packed it in it suddenly came together.

Makes 5

400g rhubarb
juice of ½ lemon
100g light honey
400ml double cream
1 vanilla pod, split in half
and seeds scraped out, or
1 teaspoon good-quality
vanilla extract
handful of pistachios, to serve

FOR THE CARAMELISED
RHUBARB
2 sticks rhubarb
thumb-sized piece of fresh
ginger, peeled and grated
olive oil
2 tablespoons soft brown sugar

1. Juice the 400g of rhubarb – the juice should come to around 200ml. Pour the juice into a small pan, bring to the boil and continue to boil until it has reduced to 100ml. While it is boiling, try to scoop off as much of the green scum that rises to the surface as possible – leaving you with a hot pink liquid. Take off the heat and add the lemon juice.

2. In a small pan over a medium heat, warm the honey and cream. Add the vanilla pod and seeds. Bring the cream mixture to the boil and boil for exactly 3 minutes, stirring occasionally. Take off the heat and pour in the rhubarb liquid, stirring them together.

3. Pour the rhubarb cream mixture into five ramekins and place them in the fridge. Leave to set for about 4 hours.

4. Meanwhile, make the caramelised rhubarb. Preheat the oven to 180°C/gas 4 and chop the rhubarb into chunks. Place the pieces in an ovenproof dish along with the ginger. Drizzle with olive oil and sprinkle with the soft brown sugar and blast in the oven for 10 minutes, until sizzling.

5. When ready to serve, remove the ramekins from the fridge. Chop the pistachios and sprinkle on top, finishing with a couple of pieces of the caramelised rhubarb.

Rose and Vanilla Cupcakes

We are not usually into overly girly things, but we are really into these…
and they are very girly. Vanilla and rose, pink and cream… how perfect.
And all in cupcake form.

1. Preheat the oven to 180°C/gas 4 and line a 12-hole muffin tin with
   paper cases.
2. Beat together the butter, caster sugar and vanilla seeds. Gradually add
   the beaten eggs, and then the yoghurt and mix until combined. Gently
   fold in the sifted flour and baking powder.
3. Spoon the cake mix into the muffin cases and bake for 20–25 minutes,
   or until golden and bouncy to touch. Transfer to a wire rack to cool.
4. Mix together the icing sugar, yoghurt and rosewater to make the icing.
   Add a drop of pink food colouring and mix in; you are looking for a
   delicate pale pink. Spoon the icing over the cupcake and decorate with
   dried rose petals or freeze-dried raspberry powder .

Makes 12

200g unsalted butter, softened
200g caster sugar
1 vanilla pod, split in half and
  seeds scraped out
4 eggs, beaten
80g natural yoghurt
200g self-raising flour, sifted
1 teaspoon baking powder
dried rose petals or freeze-dried
  raspberry powder, to decorate

FOR THE ICING
100g icing sugar, sifted
100g natural yoghurt
2 teaspoons rosewater
few drops of pink food
  colouring

You can use this recipe to make one large cake; just pour into a 20cm springform cake tin
and bake for 30–40 minutes.

Peanut Butter Cups

These little cups are pure nostalgia for us. We have memories of first discovering Reese's Peanut Butter Cups as kids … wow – the combination was quite something: the salty nut butter that was slightly gritty in texture with the sweet smooth chocolate encasing it. We now make these healthier versions for that mid-afternoon lull – they are delectable straight from the fridge with a coffee or a cup of tea. Compared to your shop-bought choccy they are full of protein and low in sugar, which means you can have two, or maybe even three…

You'll need a rubber chocolate mould to make these – rubber ice-cube trays also work well!

1. Preheat the oven to 180°C/gas 4.
2. Put the peanuts and cashews on a baking tray and roast for 15 minutes until golden – take care not to let them burn.
3. Break up the chocolate into pieces and put into a heatproof bowl. Set over a pan of simmering water, making sure the bottom of the bowl doesn't touch the water. Once melted, stir in the coconut oil.
4. Put a handful of the nuts into a food processor and blitz to make crumbs. Blitz the remaining nuts until they form a smooth butter. Add the salt, maple syrup and vanilla and blend again. Add the sesame seeds or flaxseeds and the nut crumbs and pulse to combine. Stir in the crisped rice.
5. Put a tablespoon of the chocolate mixture into each rubber mould and transfer to the fridge until almost set. Then put a blob of the peanut butter mixture on top and cover with the remaining chocolate. Put into the freezer until completely set (about 10 minutes), then transfer to the fridge, where they will keep for up to 10 days. Not that they'll last that long…

Makes 12

200g peanuts
100g cashews
200g good-quality dark chocolate
200g good-quality milk chocolate
50g coconut oil
1 teaspoon sea salt
1 tablespoon maple syrup
1 teaspoon vanilla extract
50g sesame seeds or flaxseeds
big handful of crisped rice cereal

Three Nut Coconut Bites

We can't count the times we have made health bars for photoshoots and they haven't quite worked out, being either dry and crumbling apart or just oily and too soft. This is our perfected recipe – foolproof, delicious and chewy. They're inspired by the raw health balls Jemima ate post-pregnancy, to give her an extra boost of nutrients. These bars are packed full of omega-3 fats, healthy oils and plenty of protein for energy.

1. Preheat the oven to 220°C/gas 7.

2. Put the almonds and cashews onto a baking tray, pop into the oven and roast for 5–10 minutes, giving the tray a good shake halfway through, until they are golden brown. Take out of the oven and leave to cool.

3. Put half the almonds, cashews and macadamia nuts in a food processor and blitz until chopped, then transfer to a bowl. Mix in the desiccated coconut, oats, flax powder and hemp seeds.

4. Add the remaining nuts and sunflower seeds to the food processor and blitz for 3–4 minutes to form a nut butter (you might need to stop and scrape the sides down).

5. Melt the cacao butter and coconut oil in a pan and mix in the nut butter, tahini and maple syrup. Pour into the dry mixture and stir to combine.

6. Line a 30 x 20cm tin with baking paper. Spoon the mixture into the tin and press down. Sprinkle with desiccated coconut, sesame seeds and sea salt. Place in the fridge until set, then cut into squares or bars. Keep refrigerated – these will last for up to 2 weeks.

Makes about 24 squares

100g almonds, toasted
100g cashews, toasted
150g macadamia nuts
150g desiccated coconut
100g gluten-free porridge oats
3 tablespoons flax powder
3 tablespoons hemp seeds
50g sunflower seeds
100g raw cacao butter
100g coconut oil
2 tablespoons tahini
3 tablespoons maple syrup
desiccated coconut, sesame seeds
   and sea salt for sprinkling

Larder

Jalapeño, Cashew and Avocado Dip

Serves 4–6

1 x 200g jar of jalapeños
100g basil
80g coriander
200g cashew nuts
1 avocado, stone removed
   and peeled
½ lemon
squeeze of maple syrup
salt and pepper

This is our favourite Tart dip, we've served it on so many shoots as a dip for crudités. It's great with roasted potato or sweet potato wedges and we also often serve it with some of our breakfasts, like the quinoa dish on page 38, or with a breakfast bruschetta topped with a poached egg.

1. Blitz all the ingredients together in the food processor until not quite smooth – you want it to still have some texture. Taste and adjust the seasoning.
2. This is best served straight away, but will keep in the fridge for a day.

Jalapeño, Lime and Ginger Sauce

Serves 4

3 tinned jalapeños (or about
   8 slices)
½ shallot
small bunch of coriander
5cm piece of fresh ginger, peeled
1 tablespoon honey
juice of 1 lime
salt and pepper

This is a very good tangy number that is delicious with oysters or other raw fish, such as tuna sashimi.

1. Blend all the ingredients together in a food processor until well combined. Season to taste with salt and pepper.
2. Store in an airtight container in the fridge for up to 2 days.

Yoghurt Chimichurri

Serves 4–6

bunch of parsley
bunch of coriander
1 clove garlic
3 spring onions, chopped
1 teaspoon Dijon mustard
1 tablespoon sherry vinegar
4 tablespoons olive oil
small squeeze of honey
4 tablespoons yoghurt
salt and pepper

This salsa is really good served with meats like beef, lamb or chicken.

1. Put all the ingredients into a food processor and blitz until combined but still with some texture. You may need to scrape down the sides of the bowl and blitz again.
2. Taste and season with salt and pepper. This is best served immediately, but will keep in the fridge, covered, for up to a day.

Spiced Yoghurt

Serves 4–6

1 teaspoon coriander seeds
1 teaspoon cumin seeds
250g natural yoghurt
½ tablespoon olive oil
1 clove garlic, crushed
1 lemon, zested, plus juice of ½
1 shallot, finely chopped
1 tablespoon chopped
 mint leaves
1 tablespoon chopped
 coriander leaves

We make spiced yoghurts all the time – they are really versatile, and great for using as a dressing for salads, cooked vegetables or meat. This is also a nice thing to add to the table if you are preparing a spread but want to keep the main dishes dairy free.

1. Place a small pan over a medium heat and add the coriander and cumin seeds. Toast for a few minutes until smoking, shaking the pan to stop them burning. Remove and crush in a mortar and pestle, then leave to cool.

2. Combine all the remaining ingredients, including the crushed spices, in a bowl. Serve right away, or store in the fridge until needed. This will keep in the fridge, covered, for a day.

Serves 4

200g Greek yoghurt
80g feta
2 limes, zest and juice
bunch of coriander
bunch of parsley
1 tablespoon water
2 spring onions, chopped
1 clove garlic, crushed
3 tablespoons olive oil
½ teaspoon ground cumin
salt and pepper

Yoghurt, Feta and Herb Dressing

This is great with a chunkier salad, perhaps with torn-up roast chicken and new potatoes. It also works well with crudités.

1. Put all the ingredients into a food processor and blitz until combined but still with some texture (you don't want it too smooth). You may need to scrape down the sides of the bowl and blitz again.

2. Taste and season with salt and pepper. Serve immediately, or store in the fridge, covered, for up to a day.

Serves 4

2 tablespoons tahini
2 tablespoons water
1 lime, zest and juice, plus extra
 if needed
1 tablespoon toasted sesame oil
good squeeze of runny honey
1 teaspoon peeled and grated
 fresh ginger
1 garlic clove, crushed
1 shallot, finely diced
100g toasted, chopped hazelnuts

Sweet Tahini Ginger Dressing

This is an excellent dressing for some crunchy greens, such as steamed fine green beans.

1. First mix together the tahini and water in a small bowl until you have a loose mixture (this will make it easier to add the other ingredients).

2. Whisk in the lime juice and all the remaining ingredients until well combined, add more water if needed. Use straight away, or store in the fridge, covered, for a couple of days.

Smoky Harissa

This is a Tart classic, one to make in bulk as it can be enjoyed with so many dishes (our favourite is on top of avocado toast with a poached egg). We occasionally make this as a smoked sauce, putting the tomatoes and other vegetables in the smoker to cook (see page 271). The rest of the vegetables will need double the smoking time that the tomatoes do. Then place them all into the food processor and blitz away.

Serves 6–10

10 large tomatoes (a mixture of varieties)

3 red peppers, deseeded and chopped

4 red onions, chopped

12 red finger-length chillies

handful of thyme

1 whole head of garlic

2 tablespoons olive oil

1 tablespoon coriander seeds

1 tablespoon cumin seeds

1 tablespoon caraway seeds

1 tablespoon red wine vinegar

1 tablespoon maple syrup

juice of ½ lemon

10 drops of rosewater (optional)

small bunch of coriander (optional)

salt and pepper

1. Preheat the oven to 220°C/gas 7.

2. Put the tomatoes, peppers, onions, chillies, thyme and the head of garlic into a roasting tray and drizzle with the oil. Season well with salt and pepper and give it a good mix. Roast in the oven for 30 minutes, letting it get good and smoky in the oven. The vegetables should be golden all over and almost caramelised.

3. Once you see things starting to blacken, reduce the oven temperature to 160°C/gas 3 and continue to cook for 30 minutes more. Take out and allow to cool.

4. Dry roast the coriander, cumin and caraway seeds in a dry frying pan, shaking the pan so they don't burn, then grind the seeds to a fine powder in a mortar and pestle or spice grinder.

5. Put the cooled roasted ingredients in a blender or food processor, squeezing the garlic cloves from their skins, and blitz. Add the rest of the ingredients, season well and blitz again until well combined but still with some texture.

6. Store in an airtight container in the fridge for up to 3 weeks.

Makes 2 jars

1 tablespoon groundnut oil

1 onion, thinly sliced

3 cloves garlic, chopped

3 red chillies, deseeded and finely chopped

large thumb-sized piece of fresh ginger, peeled and finely chopped

1 teaspoon cumin seeds

1 lemon grass stalk, finely chopped

500g good-quality ripe tomatoes, roughly chopped

200g soft light brown sugar

100ml white wine vinegar

25ml fish sauce

Tomato, Ginger and Chilli Chutney

This is one of our signature sauces – we serve it with so many things, from salads to curries, or even on top of eggs for brunch.

1. Heat the oil in a pan and fry the onion over a medium heat for 10–15 minutes until soft but not too coloured. Add the garlic, chillies, ginger, cumin seeds and lemon grass and cook for a further 4 minutes.

2. Add all the remaining ingredients and cook over a low heat for 45 minutes–1 hour until reduced to a thick sauce. Take off the heat and leave to cool.

3. This will keep in an airtight container in the fridge for up to 4 weeks.

Sichuan Oil

The intense, authentic Chinese flavour of this oil comes from the Sichuan peppercorns. They are dark red, strongly flavoured and tongue-numbing to eat. No store bought Chinese chilli oil can compare with the home-made version. It is one of the best recipe enhancers we know. You can serve with noodle soups, stir fries, cold noodle salads and delicious crispy bites… it could make the blandest of dishes taste good!

Serves 6–10

1 tablespoon cumin seeds

2 tablespoons crushed Sichuan peppercorns

1 small cinnamon stick

2 star anise

4 cloves

5 tablespoons groundnut oil

2.5cm piece of fresh ginger, sliced into thin rounds

2 cloves garlic, crushed

1 teaspoon chilli flakes

1 tablespoon toasted sesame oil

50g sesame seeds, toasted

2 teaspoons caster sugar

1. Dry roast the cumin seeds, Sichuan peppercorns, cinnamon stick, star anise and cloves in a frying pan until fragrant, shaking the pan so they don't burn, then grind in a spice grinder (or crush in a mortar and pestle).
2. Heat the groundnut oil in a pan over a medium heat, then add the ginger slices and, when golden (after a few minutes), add the garlic and chilli flakes   don't let the garlic burn, it should be golden.
3. Add the ground spices, which will sizzle, adding the sesame oil, toasted sesame seeds and sugar once combined. Take off the heat, leave to cool and then store in an airtight container in the cupboard – it will keep almost indefinitely.

Garlic Confit

This is a versatile and delicious condiment to have in the fridge. It works very well as a marinade, or smashed up into a dressing. Try it drizzled on a pizza or crunchy vegetables, alongside a barbecue feast, or just spread on a bruschetta, maybe with some mozzarella torn over the top.

Makes 1 jar

1 whole head of garlic, cloves peeled

olive oil

4 bay leaves

1 teaspoon dried oregano

1 teaspoon chilli flakes

1. Preheat the oven to 180°C/gas 4.
2. Place the peeled cloves into a small ovenproof dish in which they can lie in a single layer. Cover with enough olive oil to submerge the garlic completely. Add the bay leaves and put into the oven for 45 minutes.
3. Carefully remove from the oven, add the oregano and chilli flakes and leave to cool. Once cool, slightly mash up with a fork while still in the dish with the oil, then transfer the whole lot to an airtight container. Keep refrigerated for up to 2 weeks. Take out of the fridge and bring up to room temperature before using.

Walnut and Date Soda Bread

I wish we had time to cook hot crusty loaves of fresh bread every day, but sadly we don't. What we do have time for though is this quick and easy no-knead and no-fuss soda bread. It's a fantastic recipe, just the sort of thing you want to make on a Saturday morning to fill the house with the smell of freshly baked bread. It is very good toasted and used as a bruschetta, but best of all with a hunk of very good cheese.

1. Preheat the oven to 180°C/gas 4 and line a baking sheet with baking paper.
2. Mix together the flour, oats, walnuts, dates, salt and bicarbonate of soda in a large bowl and make a well in the middle.
3. Pour in the buttermilk, yoghurt and honey. Working quickly, mix everything together with your hands to form a sticky dough. Turn out onto the lined baking sheet and form into a round. Use a sharp knife to mark the bread into quarters, cutting deeply.
4. Place in the oven and cook for 50 minutes, until a hard, golden crust has formed. Remove from the oven and use a pastry brush to brush all over with melted butter. Leave to cool on a wire rack.

Makes 1 large loaf

450g mixed grain flour
50g porridge oats
50g walnuts, chopped
100g pitted dates, chopped
1 teaspoon salt
1 teaspoon bicarbonate of soda
250ml buttermilk
200ml natural yoghurt
1 tablespoon honey
butter, melted, for brushing

Flatbreads

The thought of making flatbreads might fill you with dread, but you just wouldn't believe how easy they are (well, at least with this recipe). There is no endless kneading or waiting or rising, it's a two-minute job. We use these for a lot of dishes, from dunking into a curry, as the base for a quick breakfast bruschetta, with a barbecue or as a simple pizza base (see our flatbread pizzas on page 86).

1. Put all the ingredients, except for the olive oil, into a large bowl and mix until it forms a dough – first with a spoon, then get your hands in there.

2. Dust a clean surface with flour and knead the dough for a minute or so until it forms a nice smooth ball (add more flour if needed). Cut the ball into 6–8 pieces. Dust a rolling pin with flour and roll out one of the pieces of dough as thinly as you can.

3. Place a frying pan over a high heat and add the flatbreads, one or two at a time. Cook for a couple of minutes until air pockets start to rise, then turn them over and cook again for about a minute. Take out of the pan and brush with olive oil, using a pastry brush. Repeat for the remainder of the flatbreads.

Makes 6–8

200g natural yoghurt
250g self-raising flour,
    plus extra for dusting
1 teaspoon baking powder
pinch of salt
olive oil, for brushing

If you are having these with a barbecue it's nice to add garlic, herbs and salt and pepper to the olive oil for flavour. They're also very nice with the Garlic Confit on page 260.

Fresh Pasta

Pasta has to be our Achilles heel: we love it so much we find it hard to know when to stop eating, especially when it's fresh and homemade. It's very simple and enjoyable to make – once you get the hang of it. If you're kneading by hand, you need to give it a good 10–12 minutes of love to develop the gluten, giving you a classic al dente pasta, rather than a soft, flabby one. However, we use a KitchenAid, both to make the dough and to roll the pasta, making it super-easy.

1. You can either do this all by hand, or using a food processor or KitchenAid (fitted with the dough hook). If you are working by hand, tip the flour and salt onto a clean surface and make a well in the middle, then crack the eggs into the well. Using a fork, beat the eggs and then gradually incorporate some of the flour from around the sides of the well, continuing until it has come together into one piece. Tip onto a floured surface.

2. Knead for approximately 10 minutes, until the dough becomes smooth and glossy. Roll into a ball and cover with cling film, then set aside for 30 minutes.

3. Alternatively, whizz everything together in a food processor or KitchenAid fitted with a dough hook until you have a smooth dough, then cover and set aside as above.

4. To make the pasta, cut the dough into four pieces and work each piece through a pasta machine on its widest setting, repeating a few times and occasionally folding in half. Then take the machine down to the second widest setting and repeat the rolling process. Continue adjusting the machine until you have rolled the dough through its narrowest setting. Cut in half, as it will be too long to manage by now.

5. Repeat the rolling process with the remaining pieces. Now the pasta is ready to use. You can use it to make the ravioli recipes on pages 168–170, or you can use the attachment on your pasta machine to slice it into strips to make tagliatelle. You can store the pasta by allowing it to dry out a little. To do this, hang it on a pasta dryer (or just over the back of a chair) for no more than 15 minutes (but longer if you want hard pasta to store – at least an hour). Sprinkle a little semolina over the pasta, to stop it sticking, and keep in an airtight container in the fridge for up to 2 days, or freeze for up to 2 weeks.

Serves 4

400g tipo '00' flour, plus extra
  for dusting
sea salt
4 large eggs
a little semolina, if storing

Smoking

Smoking meats and vegetables is something that we love to do and we do it a lot. We initially shied away from the technique, expecting it to be very difficult, but to our surprise we found it wasn't hard at all. Smoking gives the most wonderful depth to dishes, and once you get the hang of it it's really fun to experiment with different woodchips to create different flavours. Buying smoked food is very expensive, and a lot of the time it is dyed as well as injected with artificial flavours – so by smoking your own you know that it is 100 per cent natural. There is something primal about the process, and a huge amount of the pleasure is in the smell, leaving that wonderful bonfire incense in the air.

There are two types of smoking: hot and cold. We are talking about hot smoking here, as cold smoking is a longer, more complicated process. Hot smoking cooks the food with heat while infusing with smoke, but it is important to use a low heat; you want to create embers that smoke rather than burning the hell out of the wood, which can create an unpleasant burnt and bitter taste.

The Smoker

To create your own stove-top smoker you need to first line a roasting tray with foil. Next, spoon in 2 tablespoons of woodchips that have been soaked in water for 5 minutes. Then place a smaller baking tray on top of the woodchips (to fit inside the larger tray) to catch the fat or juices and place a wire rack over the smaller tray – this is where you will place your meat, fish or vegetables.

Lastly, cover with a lid, or tightly seal with foil. Once you have added the ingredients you are smoking (see overleaf), make sure it is tightly squished around the tray so no smoke can escape.

You can also invest in a smoker. They are inexpensive and easy to order online – we use Camerons Stovetop Smoker, which comes with a selection of woodchips.

The Burner

You can simply use your hob (gas being the best). It does create smoke, so make sure you have the extractor fan on full and the windows open, if possible.

A good tip is to use a camping stove and pop it outside your back doorstep. A smoker fits perfectly on top and it stops the kitchen getting smoky. You want to use the camp stove on the lowest heat possible.

Cooking

Once the smoker is set up and on the heat, leave it until you see wisps of smoke coming out. Then, add your ingredients in a single layer on the wire rack. Our favourite things to smoke are tomatoes and fish (see pages 111 and 116 for timings). Once everything is cooked through, remove from the heat and leave to cool.

The Woodchips

Always use untreated woodchips. Here are some of our favourites:

Alder – very delicate, perfect for fish and poultry
Apple – slightly sweet, good for pork and red meats
Beech – mild flavour and a good all-rounder, good for meat and seafood
Cherry – slightly sweet, rich and smooth, good for game, duck and vegetables
Hickory – the classic hardwood with a lot of depth, perfect for BBQ ribs or chicken
Maple – subtle flavour, good with delicate foods
Oak – the backbone of smoking flavour, good with any meat

Tips

Always cure fish or meat before smoking, either in salt or brine (we have included instructions in our recipe on page 116, but you might want to play around with other fishes once you have got the smoking knack).

Always keep on a low temperature.

Keep an eye on it, especially if you are smoking meat or fish, so as not to overcook the ingredients. If you are using a homemade smoker, peel back the foil and peek in. Once you have used the smoker a couple of times you'll have a good idea of how long things take.

Always use the freshest meat or fish.

Soak your woodchips in water beforehand for anything from 5 minutes to 1 hour; this helps keep the temperature down.

About the Authors

Lucy Carr-Ellison and Jemima Jones are the founders of Tart London, a boutique-style catering company that provides high-quality, healthy and delicious on-site cooking for fashion and film shoots and private events. Previous clients include Stella McCartney, Gucci, Lancôme and Tim Walker, and magazines such as *Vogue*, *GQ* and *Love*. Lucy and Jemima also write a weekly *ES Magazine* column in which they share some of their best-loved recipes, and are planning the opening of their own restaurant following a successful pop-up.

Thank You

Wonderful people with whom we have worked and who have supported us along the way – Tim Walker, David Sims, Stella McCartney, Ragi Dholakia and Tim Clifton-Green, Sylvia Farago, AND Productions, Ellen von Unworth, *Vogue*, *Love* magazine, Agent Provocateur.

To Tom Asquith and Ben Goldsmith for enduring all of our early morning catering wake-ups, helping us out of the door in the wee hours with prepped food, and accepting (mainly with a lot of complaints) our cooking odours upon return!

To our families, our parents and our siblings, for your encouragement and support.

Rowan Yapp, Laura Edwards, Lucy Kingett, Zoe Waldie, Tabitha Hawkins – thank you all for making this happen, it's beyond a dream and we still can't believe it is happening.

The wonderful Jackson Boxer from Brunswick House who has been more than a mentor to us over the past five years.

Purple Team especially Cat Garret and George Georgopoulos.

Laura Weir from the *Evening Standard Magazine* – thank you for giving us the opportunity of a lifetime. We love writing our column, and some of our favourite recipes that we created for the magazine are deeply ingrained in this book.

Wedgwood for making our pop-up restaurant in Queen's Park happen – without you this wouldn't have been possible.

Sevket Gokce from Parkway Greens in Camden Town, a fruit and veg genius who supplies the most amazing array of fresh produce, forever inspiring and beautiful.

April Potts – for being amazing and inspirational. Without you and Tim, Tart would never have happened.

Thank you to all of our amazing assistants who were up at the crack of dawn, worked so hard and made it so fun (even when cooking in a cupboard, a horsebox in the middle of winter or on the roof of a twenty-storey building on the hottest day of the year) – Kate, Jess, Hannah, Kat, Bev, Chloe and everyone else, you deserve a gold medal.

Index

INDEX

5 7 9 10 8 6

Square Peg, an imprint of Vintage,
20 Vauxhall Bridge Road,
London SW1V 2SA

Square Peg is part of the Penguin Random House
group of companies whose addresses can be found
at global.penguinrandomhouse.com.

Text copyright Lucy Carr-Ellison and Jemima Jones 2018
Photography © Laura Edwards 2018
Except photographs on pages 12, 13, 14, 15, 16, 17, 103, 274
are authors' own

Lucy Carr-Ellison and Jemima Jones have asserted their
right to be identified as the authors of this Work in accordance
with the Copyright, Designs and Patents Act 1988

First published by Square Peg in 2018

penguin.co.uk/vintage

A CIP catalogue record for this book is available from
the British Library

ISBN 9781910931578

Design by Julia Connolly and Kris Potter
Photography by Laura Edwards
Prop styling by Tabitha Hawkins

Printed and bound in China by C&C Offset Printing Co., Ltd

Penguin Random House is committed to a sustainable future
for our business, our readers and our planet. This book is made
from Forest Stewardship Council® certified paper.